2,002
Ways
to Cheer
Yourself Up

Books by Cyndi Haynes
and Dale Edwards

2002 Things to Do on a Date
2002 Ways to Say, "I Love You"
2002 Ways to Find, Attract, and Keep a Mate
2002 Romantic Ideas

2,002
Ways
to Cheer
Yourself Up

**Andrews McMeel
Publishing**

Kansas City

www.andrewsmcmeel.com
98 99 00 01 BIN 10 9 8 7 6 5 4 3 2 1

Library of Congress Cataloging-in-Publication Data
Haynes, Cyndi.
    2,002 ways to cheer yourself up / Cyndi Haynes.
      p.   cm.
    ISBN 0-7407-2289-1 (pbk.)
    1. Melancholy. 2. Happiness 3. Adjustment
(psychology) 4. Conduct of life. I. Title.
BF575.M44H38   1998
152.4'1—dc21   98-14285
                                                    CIP

Dear Reader,

Whether you are looking for a little diversion to cheer you up or a life-changing insight to heal your broken heart, it is my sincere wish that you will find what you are searching for within these pages.

Most warmly,
Cyndi Haynes

*For Marme, Bubba, and Annie,
who always manage to
cheer me up*

2,002 Ways to Cheer Yourself Up

*No life is so hard that you can't
make it easier by the
way you take it.*

ELLEN GLASGOW

1. Make a list of all the people you
   care about most and put your
   own name at the very top of
   the list.

2. Reach out to others for help, but
   choose your helpers wisely.

3. Put your sweet tooth to work for
   you. Yes, go out and treat yourself to a huge banana split.

4. Give your eyes a little treat. Watch the moon rise over a beautiful, calm body of water. Imagine yourself feeling that relaxed and calm.

5. Set your alarm clock for the wee hours and get up to watch the sunrise.

6. Paddle a canoe across a calm lake in the fall, so that you can enjoy a different view of the leaves changing color.

7. Make your world a little cheerier by:
   Planting flowers
   Planting a tree
   Pulling weeds
   Planting a vegetable garden

8. Throw a party that people will be talking about for years.

9. Pat yourself on the back for all the many things that you have done right in your life.

10. Count up all the miracles that have taken place in your life so far. Know that there will be even more to come!

11. Sing your blues in the shower, and let the water wash your troubles away (at least for a few relaxing minutes).

12. Take a chance and get involved again in life.

13. Learn to enjoy being by yourself, so that you will never feel lonely again.

14. The old-timers were right. You do need to take it one day at a time.

15. Go to the nearest church to light a candle and say a prayer for yourself.

16. Send out loving thoughts to your enemies.

17. If you are your own worst enemy, send loving thoughts to yourself. You may feel funny at first, but you will start to see a big difference in just a few days.

18. Don't be humble—remind yourself of all your good qualities.

19. If you're one of the brave-hearted, turn yourself upside down by working on your weaknesses.

20. Focus your attention on the good things in your life and not on the bad things.

21. It is tough to do, but give up trying to control others in your life.

22. Take charge of your speech habits. Stop saying, "If only . . ."

23. Pay off all your credit cards.

24. Understand this important tidbit of information:
     Temper tantrums
     Worry
     Grudges
     rob you of your energy.

25. Keep in mind that how you "see" the world is how it will be.

26. Listen closely to the advice of loved ones.

27. Stay in bed a half hour longer in the morning to spoil yourself.

28. Boost your self-esteem by stopping a bad habit.

29. Stop overdoing and overcommitting. Take good care of your time.

30. Attend an opening on Broadway, or someplace equally exciting.

31. Participate in a new activity at least once a week.

32. Bolster your sense of humor by reading funny, uplifting books.

Most Popular Ways to Counteract Stress:

Exercise	*Meditation*
Yoga	*Deep breathing*
Walking	*Music*

33. Pay close attention to your intuition.

34. Refrain from making snap decisions.

35. Know that there aren't any quick fixes. Learn to be patient with your heart.

36. Start your day off with a plate of yummy French toast or one of your favorite dishes.

37. Visit an Amish village and realize that there are many joys to a simple lifestyle. Maybe you need to streamline yours a little to make yourself more in control during this rocky time in your life.

38. Spread some good feelings by making homemade jam and taking a jar to each of your neighbors.

39. Go snorkeling to get a different perspective on the world.

40. Build a model dream car like the one you did as a child. Now promise yourself that one day soon you will have the real thing.

41. Spend the day acting like a tourist in your own hometown.

42. When it snows, make a snow angel to remind yourself of the guardian angel who is always looking after you.

43. Sing your favorite hymn and concentrate on the deep, spiritual meaning of the song. What does it mean to you? How does it relate to your life?

44. Take a ferryboat ride to some-place that you have never been before.

45. Toast marshmallows over a fire to feel like a kid again.

46. After a storm, look for rainbows everywhere you go.

47. Search out miracles. Once you start looking for them, you will be amazed at how many you find.

48. Ask everyone you know to tell you stories about miracles in their lives.

49. Be open to an epiphany—you may have one.

50. Dangle your feet in a nearby fountain to give yourself a case of "happy feet."

51. If you feel alone, research your family tree to regain your sense of belonging.

52. Go on an archaeological dig and see what you can learn from the past.

53. Lighten up! Kick your shoes off and go barefoot.

54. Tired of feeling sad? Scare yourself instead—tell ghost stories in front of a roaring fire.

55. Spend the whole night watching *Nick at Night* on cable television to bring back memories of a happier time in your life.

56. Work a crossword puzzle to get your mind off your troubles.

57. Clean out your attic and look for hidden treasures.

58. Reminisce with a friend or sibling about your happy childhood days.

59. Order a fabulous, party-size pizza and skip cooking dinner tonight. Better yet, make a party of it!

60. Pop popcorn in the fireplace while drinking hot cider to get a cozy, warm feeling down deep inside.

The only way to avoid
being miserable is
not to have enough leisure
to wonder whether you are
happy or not.
GEORGE BERNARD SHAW

61. Buy a parrot and teach it to say happy words and phrases.

62. Cleaning is one of the best therapies, so clean out your closet and give your old clothes to charity. Yes, giving is also one of the best therapies!

63. Need a new friend? Throw a block party and make friends with your neighbors.

64. Turn on the radio or television for a little companionship when you are by yourself and feeling sad.

65. Play a game of solitaire to fill a lonely hour or two.

66. Pamper yourself by getting a pedicure.

67. Put your blues to music. Who knows, you may just be the next B. B. King!

68. Jog along a beautiful beach and get lost in the scenery.

69. Too tired to jog? Try a horseback ride along the beach.

70. Savor any good moments that come your way.

71. Repair all the broken things around your home, as it will put you in the mind-set to repair your own broken spirit.

72. Smile at police officers—they have their own problems in today's world.

73. Make a major production out of cooking Sunday dinners.

74. Take a drive around Christmastime and get caught up in the holiday spirit.

75. Attend a benefit for a worthy cause.

76. Buy a hope chest to start planning for a brighter future.

77. Reread the best love letters you have ever received.

78. Fill a large pitcher with fresh flowers from your garden to put by your bed. You will wake up to their lovely fragrance.

79. Create a silly diversion in your daily routine.

80. For a daring change, dye your hair red.

81. Listen to self-help tapes while commuting to and from work.

82. Keep in mind the brilliant wisdom behind the old adage "When the going gets tough, the tough go shopping."

83. Want to look and feel better? Go on a diet to lose any excess weight.

84. Call an older and wiser sibling for advice.

85. Put some glamour in your life by visiting a taping of an upbeat television show at a local TV station.

86. Enter a contest—it will cheer you up tons when you win a prize.

87. Rent Walt Disney's wonderful movie *Pollyanna* and absorb its message.

88. Did you know that different foods can affect your moods differently? Eliminate unhealthy foods from your diet.

89. Be strong, be brave, and take control of your life.

90. Want to keep your mind occupied and improve your financial skills? Take an hour to balance your checkbook.

91. Spend an afternoon just acting silly for a change. In a few hours, you will feel like a new person.

92. Even if you don't feel like it, put on a big smile. It takes fewer muscles to smile than to frown!

93. This is a biggie! Give up the old habit of complaining.

94. Stop being a couch potato.

95. Wear a totally outrageous outfit that is unlike the old, depressed you. Shock yourself into happiness.

96. When times get really hard, learn to live moment to moment.

97. Spend fifteen minutes a day learning a foreign language you've always wanted to speak.

98. Keep in mind that when God closes a door, He always opens a window somewhere.

99. Read, read, read. Books can be one of the biggest contributors to the success of your life.

Self-pity is our worst enemy, and if we yield to it, we can never do anything wise in the world.
HELEN KELLER

100. Need to feel spiritual? Try a trip to the Holy Land.

101. If the above trip is a little too far, travel to Sedona, Arizona.

102. Remember that you can't be brave if you have only good things happen to you.

103. When you get to the end of your rope, make a knot and hang on.

104. Take up ballroom dancing and concentrate on your feet instead of your problems.

105. Reread your favorite childhood book before you drift off to sleep.

106. Take a minivacation by staying over at a friend's house this weekend.

107. Order a gift for yourself from a mail-order catalog and look forward to its arrival.

108. Spend a weekend on a houseboat to experience a change of pace.

109. Pause on the hour to listen to the beautiful sound of church bells pealing.

Ways to Gain Perspective
on your Troubles:

Talk with friends
Chat with family members
Talk to a professional counselor
Call your doctor
Visit with your cleric

110. Raid your refrigerator late at night. Go hog-wild!

111. Watch the moonlight sparkle on freshly fallen snow.

112. Are you having trouble sleeping? Curl up on satin sheets tonight.

113. Have a happy tomorrow. Do your emotional homework *today*.

114. Know that life is going on all around you—don't wait to get on with it.

115. Food for thought: In two days, tomorrow will be yesterday.

116. Allow others to help you.

117. Invite friends over for a visit on a regular basis, even when your heart isn't in it.

118. Daydream only happy dreams. Give up those melodramas.

119. Throw a pity party for yourself.

120. Did you play sports as a kid? Then this Saturday head over to the park and play again.

121. Watch the movie *It's a Wonderful Life*, starring Jimmy Stewart.

122. Escape to a spa. Yes, sometimes you can run from your troubles.

123. Look for ways to bring a sense of closure to your troubles.

Great Cheer-up Foods:
Hot flavored tea
Hot cocoa
Steaming bowl of vegetable soup
Homemade cookies
Box of chocolates

124. Lighten up!

125. Try to view your life as one big adventure.

126. Learn to laugh at yourself.

127. Attend a fashion show and pick out a fabulous new outfit.

128. Pray in a huge cathedral.

129. Plant a garden and get back to nature, at least in a little way.

130. Feed the birds in the wintertime.

131. Get a new attitude. After all, the old one isn't working or you wouldn't be reading this book!

132. Dine at your favorite restaurant tonight. Don't wait for a special occasion.

133. If your home is filled with painful memories, consider moving.

134. Cry on your dad's shoulder.

135. Cry on your mom's shoulder.

136. Call a long-lost friend. Old friends are often the best friends.

137. Ask for a raise. When one area of your life improves, you will feel better everywhere.

138. Make definite plans for your immediate future.

139. Say grace before each meal.

140. Whistle while you work. Hey, it worked for the dwarfs!

141. Take your brown-bag lunch to a scenic spot.

142. Spend at least thirty minutes a day outside in the fresh air.

143. Look for the angels among us.

144. Find a four-leaf clover for luck.

145. Take a twenty-minute nap each afternoon until you get your strength back.

146. Rearrange your furniture to create a fresh home environment.

147. Write to Santa and tell him how you would like your life to be next year at this time.

148. Visit a warm climate during January or February to help cure your wintertime blues.

149. Flirt with an attractive stranger on safe ground.

150. Ask for some time off from work.

151. Paint the town red this coming Saturday night.

152. Ask your oldest friend to psycho-analyze you. What message do you hear?

153. Start your day off on a light note by reading the comics.

154. Open your windows and let some fresh air into your home.

155. Experiment with life.

156. Learn from life.

157. Dress up to stay at home.

158. Turn your troubles over to God.

159. If you are having trouble sleeping or are feeling tense, give up caffeine.

160. Walk a country mile on a summer's day.

161. Fill up your lonely hours with volunteer work.

162. Cheat on your diet, just this once!

163. Spend one whole day being lazy.

164. Tune in to your favorite television drama and be glad that you don't have those troubles to contend with in your life.

165. Take a brisk, early-morning walk to clear your head.

166. Give yourself a flower-of-the-month membership, so that you will have beautiful flowers all year long to brighten up your spirits.

167. Want a fun pick-me-up gift? Give a friend a certain amount of money and ask her to get you a wonderful surprise.

168. Make yourself absolutely indispensable to someone in this world.

169. Memorize affirmations of hope and repeat them at bedtime.

170. Watch Jay Leno or David Letterman for a late-night laugh.

171. Get "comfy" as often as you can.

172. Give thanks for every single one of your blessings.

173. Climb a tree. You'll feel like a child again.

174. Be decadent—don't make your bed before you go off to work.

175. Go sailing and feel the wind in your face, blowing your troubles right out of your head.

176. Play a good-natured prank on a friend. Fun always lifts your spirits.

177. Attend a church supper. Being in the presence of other believers will bring you a sense of belonging and comfort.

178. Practice looking on the bright side of life.

179. This is a biggie: Forgive those who have wronged you.

180. Watch a little girl care for her beloved doll.

181. Invite a neighbor over for an impromptu dinner.

> *Experience is not*
> *what happens to you,*
> *it is what you do*
> *with what happens to you.*
>
> ALDOUS HUXLEY

182. Want to feel the warm fuzzies? Watch *Lassie* reruns.

183. Visit the children's ward at a local hospital. Afterward, your troubles won't seem nearly so bad.

184. Make a list of all your good qualities. Don't be modest here. This will boost your self-esteem and your spirits.

185. Fluff your pillows before going to bed. You need to pamper yourself in even the smallest ways.

186. Pray nightly.

187. Go on a major shopping spree.

188. Give yourself permission to get on with your life.

189. Tell yourself that it is good to get on with your life. Give up your feelings of guilt.

190. Nibble on animal crackers while sipping a piping hot cup of cocoa.

191. When it is fall in your hemisphere of the world, travel to a distant hemisphere that is celebrating springtime.

192. OK, get this! Today *really* is the first day of the rest of your life.

193. Rent all your favorite videos.

194. Find religion.

195. Give yourself someone to love.

196. Scratch your dog's tummy and ears. At least *he* will be happy.

197. Take a few hours on a beautiful day to just lie in a hammock and watch the clouds roll by.

198. Make someone else feel valuable.

199. Force yourself to greet each day with a smile.

200. Get a checkup, as it could be a physical problem that is causing your blues.

201. Subscribe to *Guideposts* magazine for a real spirit booster.

202. Refrain from focusing on your problems to the exclusion of the rest of your life.

203. Practice empathy for others—it's the exact opposite of self-preoccupation.

Great Escape Activities:

Reading romance novels
Devouring a box of chocolates
Traveling
Getting a pet
Watching action movies
Window-shopping

204. Good news: Most emotional damage is reversible.

205. Stop trying to live other people's lives.

206. Treat yourself with patience and kindness.

207. Never exaggerate your troubles to yourself. You want to make them smaller, not larger.

208. Know when to say yes.

209. Learn when to say no.

210. Bask in the affection of your friends.

211. Affirm your successes, even the smallest ones.

212. Surround yourself with beautiful things.

213. Ask yourself if you are suffering from a case of heartache or a clinical depression. If you are suffering from depression, seek professional help.

214. To relieve stress, try biofeedback.

215. Keep in mind that full recovery from a major loss may take a year or more. Relax!

216. Understand that one of the great keys to a happy life is balance.

217. Consider taking up expressive forms of dance to work out your negative emotions.

218. When you are ready to make changes, be sure that you are making positive ones.

219. Keep a self-improvement chart or diary.

220. Practice positive imagery to create a happier world for yourself.

221. Meditate to regain your sense of peace and tranquillity. It is one of the world's oldest techniques for emotional healing.

222. Remember that you can't solve all your problems at once.

223. Keep your world open to new and exciting experiences.

224. Talk about health and happiness.

225. Build relationships based on trust, so that your true feelings can emerge.

226. Keep in mind that no one can make you happy except you.

227. Stop romanticizing the past.

228. Find the "flow" in your life and get into it.

229. Taking a business trip? Go to a church while you are traveling and pray.

230. If your self-esteem is a little shaky, attend a Dale Carnegie course.

231. After the next snowfall, dig up your old sled and have fun no matter what your age.

232. Gaze up at the stars and realize that in the vast universe your problems probably look very small.

233. Set a festive table with a centerpiece and pretty table linens, even if you are dining by yourself.

234. This one works every time: Play with your dog.

235. Plan an elegant dinner party that would make Martha Stewart proud. Keep your mind occupied with making all the arrangements.

236. Write all your painful feelings in a diary.

237. Relax in a whirlpool tub.

238. Force yourself to do some things on your "To Do" list.

239. If you have a broken heart, place a Band-Aid over it to remind yourself symbolically that it will heal as all your wounds have in the past.

240. Figure out what your loneliest times are and make plans to fill those lonely hours.

241. Learn to play a musical instrument, as music is good for the soul.

242. Need a hug? Go to your nearest toy store and buy a wonderful Steiff teddy bear to hug to your heart's content.

243. Have a gourmet picnic in front of your television set tonight instead of eating alone in your kitchen.

244. Need a diversion? Then head to the video arcade and spend an hour playing some high-tech games.

245. Unlock the magic—enjoy an Oreo cookie and milk.

246. People-watch while strolling along a busy boardwalk.

247. Read the works of the world's great philosophers.

248. Plan for your future by starting an IRA. At least you won't have to worry about retirement.

249. Take a self-defense class to boost your confidence.

250. Buy a ton of junk food and invite your closest friends over for an old-time slumber party.

251. Enjoy a glass of brandy in front of a roaring fire.

252. When you look good, you feel good, so have your hair styled by a top-notch stylist.

This is the true joy in life, the being used for a purpose recognized by yourself as a mighty one.

GEORGE BERNARD SHAW

253. Wangle an invitation to your best friend's house for dinner.

254. Write a poem expressing your feelings.

255. Spend a few moments on a beautiful fall evening enjoying a harvest moon while contemplating the meaning of life.

256. Read the latest motivational books.

257. Cultivate new dreams for yourself. Make sure they are big and bold dreams—you deserve the very best.

258. Now is the time to empty your childhood piggy bank and buy yourself a special gift.

259. Drink a glass of warm milk at bedtime.

260. If you have trouble falling asleep, spray a little lavender cologne on your pillow. It will help you to fall fast asleep.

261. Try to brighten up even the tiniest corners of your world. Place helpful quotes on pot holders, in a briefcase, and even on your steering wheel.

262. Remind yourself that even with all your troubles, there are still people who would love to have your life.

263. After a hard day, stop by a country inn for some herbal tea.

264. Spend a Saturday afternoon at —yes—a bowling alley. It is too loud in there to even hear yourself think, so you will forget your troubles.

The best cure for worry,
depression, melancholy, brooding
is to go deliberately forth
and try to lift with one's sympathy
the gloom of somebody else.

ARNOLD BENNETT

265. Take your vitamins. Yes, your mother was right all along!

266. Carry your loved ones' pictures in your wallet, so that you can look at them often when you feel alone.

267. Get back to nature by going camping.

268. Indulge your sweet tooth with a large chocolate cheesecake smothered in strawberries.

269. Start a new career or business.

270. Share a little piece of yourself:
Give away your best-kept secret
recipe.

271. Learn to use your time wisely.

272. Write your troubles in the sand
on a beautiful beach and watch
them disappear.

273. Invite a friend to lunch today.

274. Have yourself paged out of any
social situation that you know
will be painful and unpleasant
for you.

275. Give yourself a kiss—a Hershey
Kiss, that is—and throw in a bag
of Hugs for good measure.

276. If you need to, learn to eat
humble pie.

277. Live by the motto "Never complain, never explain."

278. Wear brightly colored clothes.

279. Lose yourself in the latest fad.

280. Sleep under a thick down comforter so you will feel as snug as a bug in a rug.

281. Do you love babies? Then spend lonely hours helping a teenage mother.

282. Put a lock on your bedroom door, to secure some quality private time to get your thoughts in order.

283. Kiss away a child's hurts.

284. Go to a double feature, for twice the distraction from your worries.

285. Allow yourself to feel your strong unpleasant emotions.

286. Need some romance back in your life? Then go on a second honeymoon.

287. Let out your frustrations in a good old-fashioned snowball fight.

288. Want to see some order in this crazy world? Attend a dog obedience trial.

289. Be faithful to your heart.

290. In times of crisis, people draw close together, so don't foolishly build any walls.

291. Study feng shui, the ancient Chinese art of placement, to create more balance and flow in your environment.

292. Ask yourself what your hopes for the future are.

293. Learn to accept your shortcomings.

294. What you can't change, accept.

295. Know that a trouble shared is a trouble split in half.

296. Animals are great producers of joy, love, and happiness. So head on over to a friend's farm or kennel.

297. Free your life of as much anxiety as you can.

298. Drink alcohol only in moderation.

299. Too much time on your hands? Stop loafing and get busy changing your little corner of the world.

300. Head to a superstore and buy yourself some jumbo-size bags of your favorite candy.

301. Find at least one good reason to carry on in this world.

302. Get yourself into great physical shape.

303. Using a stethoscope, listen to how strongly your heart beats even when it is broken.

304. Look for the heart and soul behind every stranger's eyes.

305. In spite of your troubles, be a nice guy. Nice guys really do finish first.

306. Learn from your past mistakes, then move on with your life.

307. Believe that God has a plan for your life.

308. Rent the movie *Dead Poets Society*. It has a wonderful message that just might touch your heart.

309. Need a change of scenery but not sure what kind? Rent an RV and see the entire country. By the end of your trip, you'll have a whole new outlook on life.

310. Never believe that your life has to be perfect before you can be happy. There are inmates in prison who are happy!

311. Stand up for your rights.

312. Wear a pretty bed jacket to bed to keep yourself warm on nights when you feel a little bit lonely.

313. Do corny little gestures for your friends to show them how much you care about them.

> *Good, to forgive;*
> *Best, to forget!*
> ROBERT BROWNING

314. Give your shoulder to a friend to cry on and you'll feel better too.

315. Make a decision to be happy from this very moment forward!

316. Adopt a pet from a local animal shelter. You will be saving a life and giving yourself someone to love at the same time.

317. If you are a senior and want a pet, contact the Ralston Purina Company about their Pets for People program.

318. Coax your mom into inviting you over for Sunday supper.

319. Enjoy reading one of Mary Engelbreit's wonderful and charming little books.

320. Face your fears.

321. Get a great night's sleep by sleeping in a feather bed.

322. Take an adventurous ride in a hot-air balloon. The world looks different from way up there in the great blue yonder.

323. Watch a parade and get caught up in the excitement of the crowd.

324. Visit with people from different cultures to get a different "take" on your situation.

325. Act like a kid again by playing on a playground.

326. Have a crush on someone?
     Ask that person out for a date.

327. Start a new collection: dolls,
     trains, Limoges boxes, antiques,
     etc. New interests bring a great
     deal of enjoyment to your life.

328. Begin writing a new chapter in
     your life.

329. Turn yourself into a doer type
     of person.

330. Buy a great-looking pair of
     sunglasses to hide your
     bloodshot eyes.

331. Even if you don't feel up to it, dec-
     orate your home for the holidays.
     After you have completed the
     task, you'll be glad that you did it.

332. Send yourself a bouquet of
     flowers at work.

333. Start a rigorous exercise routine. You'll be too tired to be sad. (Be sure to check with your doctor beforehand.)

334. Before you get out of bed tomorrow morning, stretch to relax your body.

335. Every night make plans for the next day, to be sure that you stay nice and busy.

336. Spend more time at the office. Who knows, you may end up with a raise or a promotion!

337. Soak in a bubble bath while sipping champagne.

338. If you feel like crying, cry into a beautiful linen handkerchief.

339. Join a book club and spend your nights curled up with great reads.

340. Hug your Raggedy Ann doll. After all, she's the only doll with a heart.

341. On a cold, lonely night, take a cup of hot chocolate to bed with you to warm up your spirit.

342. Visit a cemetery and realize that these are the *only* people without problems.

343. Buy an eye mask to soothe your tired, crying eyes.

344. Let yourself cry when you feel like it.

345. Believe that your heart will mend.

346. Join a self-help group. If you can't find one, start one.

347. Look expectantly to the future.

348. Spend the night in your childhood home. Enjoy the warm feelings that it brings back to you.

349. Stick to your budget. You don't
need any financial troubles.

350. Dine at a Chinese restaurant and
believe any good news that your
fortune cookie tells you.

351. Listen to the song "Tomorrow"
from the musical *Annie* to get a
hopeful feeling about the future.

352. Take a cruise to an exotic locale
to forget your troubles.

*It isn't the load
that weighs you down,
it's the way you carry it.*

AUTHOR UNKNOWN

353. Watch the sun set over the ocean and marvel at how wondrous the world really is.

354. If you long for some excitement and nightlife, pack your bags and head to Las Vegas for a long weekend.

355. Ask your friends what they would do if they were in your shoes.

356. Plant a vegetable garden and give your homegrown goodies to the needy in your community.

357. Pray before you get out of bed each morning for strength to get through the day.

358. Go to a jazz club and get lost in the music.

359. Be like Susan Lucci, and practice grace under pressure.

360. Share your deep, dark secret
with your:

Minister
Therapist
Trusted friend

361. Wash your troubles right out
of your life—or at least out of
your hair. Shampoo your hair
in rainwater.

362. Sleep on your heartaches,
because things always look
better in the morning.

363. Choose your thoughts carefully,
as they will greatly determine the
quality of your entire life.

*I had no shoes and complained
until I met a man who
had no feet.*

AUTHOR UNKNOWN

364. If you believe that you will recover from this setback in your life, you will. On the other hand, if you think that you won't, you probably are right.

365. Live your own vision of your life, not your parents', not your spouse's, and certainly not your friends'.

366. Stop the habit of procrastination now. This is not the time to get stuck in a rut.

367. If you live in a crowded city, give yourself a break by heading to a quiet little town for a slow-paced weekend.

368. Visit a fabulous foreign city:

Cairo	Rome
Sydney	Quebec City
Istanbul	Rio de Janeiro

369. Deeply desire happiness for yourself.

370. Never try to fool yourself.

371. If you break down and cry in public, it is no big deal. So have these famous folks:

    Bill Clinton
    Richard Nixon
    Lou Gehrig
    George Washington

372. Give up the habit of thinking only in black and white. Some of your problems might fall into the gray area.

373. Hold a newborn baby.

374. Turn challenges into stepping-stones to recovery.

375. Ask your family doctor for suggestions on what might make you feel better.

376. Learn to relax.

377. Go out for a special midweek dinner at an upbeat restaurant.

378. Take a different route to and from work to break your daily routine.

379. Learn life's lessons so that you won't have to repeat them.

380. Give up mind reading. Ask others what they think and feel.

381. Look for the progress that you have made on your road back from heartache and hurt. Don't expect your recovery to be easy.

382. Give yourself the birthday gift that you have been wanting for a very long time.

383. Ask yourself if any personal limitations are holding you back on your road to cheering up. If so, get to work on changing them.

384. Try to be happy about others' good fortune.

385. Take a vacation that lasts an entire season.

386. Stop trying to keep a stiff upper lip. Your spirits will lift sooner if you express your emotions.

387. Sit alone in a quiet room and listen to your heart. What do you hear?

388. Try to have more fun than sadness in your life.

389. Perform an act of kindness for a stranger. Consider doing it in secret.

390. Eat plenty of veggies and fruit. You'll look better and feel better.

391. Keep in mind that jealousy will not help anyone, especially you!

392. Look into the mirror at your own two eyes and send yourself much love.

393. Dance in the summer rain.

394. Get close to Mother Nature:
    Feel the wind in your hair
    Go barefoot and feel the
        grass between your toes
    Enjoy the sun on your face
    Smell the air after a summer
        shower

395. Say a prayer whenever you feel that your spirits are starting to get lower.

396. Look at your situation from the point of view of your:
      Spouse
      Parent
      Children
      Friends
      Coworkers
      Minister

397. Plan your future with the help of a wise and trusted friend.

398. Listen to the beautiful music of one of these great composers:
      Mozart
      Stravinsky
      Messiaen
      Copland
      Bach

399. Seize the happy moments of your day and make the most of them.

400. When you watch television, view only positive and upbeat programs.

401. Help a dog or cat give birth and get caught up in the miracle of life.

402. Be wary of advice from the trendy gurus of the day.

403. If you ask someone for help and he refuses, keep asking till you find someone who is willing to help you.

404. Think prosperity instead of adversity.

405. If you feel angry, find a positive
     way to express it—for example:
     Punch a pillow
     Yell and scream in a cave
     Run
     Play a tough game of
       racquetball

406. Even at your lowest moments,
     refrain from belittling yourself.

407. Don't let others belittle you just
     because you are feeling a little
     shaky right now.

408. Make a list of ways to pamper
     yourself, and then start doing
     them.

409. If you find yourself putting on
     extra weight because of eating
     during stressful times, start a low-
     fat diet.

410. Give up making wishes.
     Instead, set goals.

411. Snuggle with your dog on a
     cold, lonely night.

412. Learn to accept compliments.

413. Even during your worst moments
     there are wonderful things hap-
     pening in the world. Keep your
     eyes wide open to see them.

414. Get lost in doing mindless
     work, such as:
     Laundry
     Weeding your garden
     Housework
     Darning

415. Make a list of ten people in
     worse shape than you, to gain a
     little perspective on your life.

416. If you are broke, don't let that stop you from going shopping. Just take yourself out window-shopping.

417. Pray with your head bowed.

> *Man is born broken.*
> *He lives by mending.*
> *The grace of God is glue.*
> EUGENE O'NEILL

418. Invent something to help make the world a better place in which to live.

419. Have your home or even one room decorated with the help of a professional interior decorator.

420. Spend a Sunday afternoon listening to a concert in the park.

421. Order a milk shake with your burger.

422. Pig out at a family-style restaurant.

423. Fly a kite on a windy day.

424. Drive backcountry roads in the fall to enjoy the beautiful foliage.

425. Host a wine-and-cheese party in honor of your triumphant spirit.

426. Make yourself some freshly squeezed lemonade.
(See, good things really do come out of lemons!)

427. Look up old friends from your past.

428. Visit with an elderly neighbor.

429. Meander through a country garden.

430. Wear your favorite cologne every day of the week—don't save it just for special occasions.

431. Go to a theme park and show yourself a wild time.

432. Take a spring break, like the one you had in school.

433. Become a go-getter.

434. See if blondes really do have more fun—dye your hair this weekend.

435. Take up a new and very strenuous sport, such as:
    Mountain climbing
    Marathon running
    Racquetball
    Weight lifting

436. Let yourself fall madly in love.

437. Keep up your family traditions. It will make your life seem more stable and secure.

438. Attend all the social affairs you are invited to that sound enjoyable.

439. Prepare a special meal for your family. If you are alone, prepare one for your friends or neighbors.

440. Every morning, tell yourself that you are getting better and better.

441. On cold nights that seem a little lonely, wrap yourself up in a beautiful antique quilt.

442. Burn scented candles to add a nice, cozy touch to your home.

443. When dining out alone, carry a good book for company.

444. Plan business lunches to keep your mind occupied during your "free" time at the office.

445. Feeling stressed? Take a long hot shower.

446. Get a membership to a trendy health club. The exercise will make you feel better and you might make some new friends.

447. Join an exercise class. It will force you to exercise on a regular basis.

448. Network, and keep up with what is going on in your career world.

449. Treat yourself to a stunning piece of gold jewelry.

450. Do little smiling exercises through-out the day. Look up and smile just for the fun of it.

451. Dig out your old sleeping bag and go sleep up in the mountains tonight.

452. When you can't sleep, do a yucky chore. In the morning you will be glad it's done.

453. Indulge your quirks.

454. Plan a little surprise for yourself, even if it is as simple as buying a box of Cracker Jack.

455. Attend great art exhibits at local galleries and museums. They will be a feast for your eyes and your soul.

456. Bake bread and enjoy the wonderful aroma.

457. When you feel stressed, calm yourself down by taking slow, deep, cleansing breaths.

Make a "Cheer-up" Basket
for a Friend That Includes:
a linen hankie
a box of tissues
a Bible
a greeting card
a teddy bear
a novel
Homemade goodies

458. Spend the day mountain climbing.

459. Looking through a telescope, pick out the brightest star and make a wish on it.

460. Go somewhere you have never been.

461. Become a light in someone else's world.

462. Try to understand the heart's lesson from *The Wizard of Oz*.

463. Read the children's classic *The Little Engine That Could*.

464. Cry along to "I'm So Lonesome I Could Cry," by Hank Williams Sr.

465. Turn your negatives into positives by looking for solutions for your troubled spots.

I'll match my flops with anybody's, but I wouldn't have missed 'em. Flops are a part of life's menu, and I've never been a girl to miss out on any of the courses.

Rosalind Russell

466. Learn to say, "I can," instead of, "I can't."

467. Fall asleep snuggled up to someone you love.

468. Finger paint your negative emotions.

469. Believe that your individual talents are gifts that you need to put to good use.

470. Throw a pebble into a pond and watch the ripples. Your life is like that as it touches others and produces its own ripple effect.

471. Learn to be God's vehicle.

472. Carry fresh and different cloth hankies for each day of the week.

473. Go back to your old hometown for a long and relaxing weekend.

474. Get a fun, part-time job to fill up some lonely hours.

475. Head to the pet store and get some goldfish to keep you company when you can't have a cat or a dog.

476. Make a Dairy Queen run late at night for a Blizzard treat—at least your tummy will be happy.

477. Fill your home with lovely green plants. It is good to be surrounded by lots of living things.

478. Ask your travel agent to plan a once-in-a-lifetime type of trip for you.

479. Call up your real estate agent and rent a vacation home.

480. Purchase a wonderful piece of art that speaks to your soul.

481. Be sure to schedule lots of activities on the weekends.

*Inside myself is a place
where I live all alone,
and that's where you renew
your springs that never dry up.*
PEARL BUCK

482. Be spontaneous. It is a sign of a healthy personality.

483. Invite someone to spend the weekend with you as a houseguest.

484. Pay strict attention to what you focus your thoughts on.

485. Show up places in style. Hire a limousine to get you to important engagements.

486. Pretend you are having a mid-life crisis—get a red sports car.

487. Call Dial-A-Prayer during a tough moment.

488. Hug your friends often.

489. Fix a light supper and then tuck yourself into bed for an early evening under the covers.

490. Read a joke book.

491. Regularly attend midweek church services.

492. Avoid egotistical people.

493. Keep away from critical and negative advice givers.

494. Walk everywhere you go—the exercise and fresh air will do you a world of good.

495. Take your morning coffee break with a compassionate coworker instead of spending it alone.

496. Seek out the type of help that you know, in your heart of hearts, you need.

497. If you think you have it rough, visit:

    A nursing home
    A prison
    An orphanage

498. Take your parents out to dinner and open up your heart to them.

499. Sleep on flannel sheets in the winter to give yourself a warm, cozy feeling even if you are alone.

500. Keep in mind that out of pain come some of life's greatest blessings.

501. If you feel sad, picture your life in the future without the pain you are now experiencing.

502. Give up whining. Your friends and family will listen to your troubles more if you have a pleasing tone of voice.

503. Watch what you say. Your subconscious will react to your words.

504. Place God in the number-one spot in your heart.

505. If you feel that you can't stand up for yourself at this time in your life, take an assertiveness training class.

506. It's tough, but try to *welcome* change.

507. Listen to Mariah Carey's song "Hero" to give yourself a little courage.

508. Accept the fact that any large change brings with it tons of smaller changes. Try to prepare yourself for all the changes coming your way.

509. Move closer to your family.

510. Even if you can't have a story-book ending, you can have a storybook setting by visiting Carmel, California.

511. Live in the present moment when you find it too painful to take life even one day at a time.

512. Refrain from settling for less than you deserve in order to stop your pain.

513. Before you go to any friends or family members with your heartache, go to God.

514. Start the day with a nice, healthy breakfast.

515. Don't yearn for what *was* in your life.

516. Snuggle up with your old child-hood teddy bear.

517. Develop your faith in God.

518. Next step: Develop faith in yourself.

519. Subscribe to *Success* maga-zine and learn how others have changed their lives in positive ways.

520. Take up a creative outlet such as:
  Painting
  Dancing
  Needlework
  Writing

521. Feeling sad? Head to McDonald's and order a Happy Meal.

522. Anytime something good happens in your life, try to magnify it in your mind to make your life seem even brighter.

Sometimes the best gain is to lose.
AUTHOR UNKNOWN

523. Keep a dream journal. It is good to know what your subconscious is working on while you are sleeping.

524. Practice random acts of kindness on *yourself!*

525. Look at your old baby pictures for a good laugh.

526. Understand that by taking control of your thoughts, you begin to shape your world for the better.

527. Live by your conscience if you want to have peace of mind.

528. Be extra nice and kind to animals. You will get so much love in return.

529. Practice what you preach by putting your new, positive ideas to work for you in every area of your life.

530. Buy a new outfit in your favorite color.

531. Don't just react to your predicament; learn to act with great forethought.

532. Have at least one good belly laugh each day.

533. Learn from trees. Yes, trees. They bend in a storm; they don't break.

534. Forget your troubles by becoming a caregiver for a hospice patient.

535. Attend a wonderful high school musical.

536. Make your mental health a top priority.

537. Don't worry about fixing others; fix yourself.

538. Set up a lot of calm moments for yourself throughout each day.

539. Eat lots of healthy, home-cooked dinners instead of rushing through a drive-through line for takeout.

540. Help those who are less fortu-nate than you.

541. Act as if you are happy, not the way you're really feeling. In time, you will begin to feel happier.

542. Do you think that your luck can't change? Look at what these people used to do for a living:

    Warren Beatty—dishwasher
    Ralph Lauren—tie salesman
    Rod Stewart—grave digger

543. Watch your temper, because when you hurt, your temper may flare.

Ways to Cheer Up Children:
Hug them
Listen to what they are saying
Reassure them
Set an example for them
Allow them to cry
Tell them it is okay to feel sad

544. Take a ride on an elephant or a camel for a great change of pace. Okay, you might have to travel for this one, but, honestly, it will be worth it!

545. Know that with God's help even this heartache will make you into a better person.

546. Yes, there is a road to happiness, or at least a street with that name in Ohio!

547. Cultivate having a thankful heart. You won't be nearly so heartbroken if you try this one.

548. Fill up your emptiness in healthy ways.

549. Stop yourself from overanalyzing your troubles.

550. Look for your:
    Inner beauty
    Joy
    Strength
    Faith

551. Allow others to give to you of their time, love, support, and friendship.

552. Study psychology.

553. Give a couple of hugs
each day.

554. Get a couple of hugs each day.
Don't hesitate to ask for them if
you have to. Just be sure to
receive some every single day.

555. Empty your mind of any emotions that you no longer need.

556. Forget your troubles by viewing
the national AIDS quilt.

557. Start an impromptu sing-along.

558. Tomorrow morning, begin the
journey of your new life.

559. Be bold in life. You aren't walking
on eggshells.

560. Find your inner sense of resilience.
You have one, you know!

561. Practice the art of self-assurance.

562. Leave cheerful greetings on all your friends' voice mail.

563. If you are alone on a Saturday night, take yourself out for a nice dinner or a movie.

564. Treat yourself as you would a special friend. After all, you should be your own best friend.

565. Act as if you're the important person that you are.

566. Face your troubles squarely.

567. Get some irons in the fire to get your life back on track.

568. Time and time again, imagine yourself feeling wonderful.

569. Become an expert at something.

570. Give yourself the care and attention that you deserve.

571. Create a firm schedule for your life until you're back on your feet.

572. Don't expect too much from friends and family. Learn to be grateful for any help that you receive.

573. Create some funky doodle art.

574. Try to produce good feelings in others. Spreading happiness always comes back to you.

575. Know that it is never too late to start over.

576. Don't allow others' opinions of how you are doing to form your self-esteem.

577. Stop measuring your success in life by others' lifestyles.

578. Gauge your life by what is in your heart, not the amount in your bank account.

579. Think light. Think free. Clear the *gunk* from your head.

580. Listen to a comedy CD.

581. Believe that worry truly is a useless emotion.

582. Read through your current diary to look for ways to improve your thinking.

583. Pretend that all is right in your world. In time it will be.

Nothing is all wrong.
Even a clock that has
stopped running is right
twice a day.

AUTHOR UNKNOWN

584. Brush the cobwebs from
your mind.

585. If the evening news gets you
down, turn it off.

586. Go for a ride on a Ferris wheel.

587. Never allow yourself to get bored.

588. Do what you loved to do as
a child.

589. Baby-sit. Children, and especially
babies, are great cheerer-uppers.

590. Look brave and bold—wear red.

591. Buy yourself a beautiful birthday cake from the finest bakery in town, even if it isn't your birthday.

592. Throw on your favorite pair of sneakers before you head to the office.

593. Call your favorite teacher and have a heart-to-heart talk.

594. Set up an appointment with your school or office counselor.

595. Need some extra help? Call your local chapter of the Mental Health Association for its list of helpful professionals and self-help groups.

596. Cultivate the powerful emotion of hope.

597. Set realistic expectations for yourself.

598. Limit your introspective moments if they put you in a gloomy frame of mind.

599. Limit the amount of time you spend alone.

600. Start a chart of your worst times throughout each day to see if there is a pattern that you can break by changing your routine.

601. Take up a noble cause, such as:
     Human rights
     Animal rights
     Children's rights
     Religious missions

602. Treat yourself to your favorite meal when you dine at a fabulous restaurant.

603. Make videotapes of your favorite old home movies to watch during lonely moments.

604. Eat a cool ice cream treat on a hot summer day.

605. Preserve your old family photographs, so you'll have a sense of where you come from.

606. Read through an old church hymnal for inspiration.

607. Win a prize for your child at a fall fair.

608. Watch the first snowfall of the season with a sense of wonder.

609. Turn off all the lights, sit under your Christmas tree, and get caught up in the holiday spirit.

610. Give yourself a minivacation. Get lost on purpose in a trendy section of your city.

611. Don't use any of your convenient appliances for at least a day to get a different perspective on how easy you have it in the late 1990s.

612. Sip a glass of hot cider with a cinnamon stick in front of a roaring fire.

613. Keep up your strength by fixing a nutritious afternoon snack.

In helping others,
we shall help ourselves,
for whatever good we give out
completes the circle
and comes back to us.
FLORA EDWARDS

614. Follow your heart, but make sure your head approves.

615. Throw yourself into your hobbies to create more fun in your life.

616. Call in *well* to work—take a day off if you're allowed.

617. Take a mental-health vacation or at least a mental-health weekend.

618. Become a Lamaze coach for a single mom.

619. Read your old comic books.

620. Marvel at the little rainbows formed by crystal prisms.

621. If you feel lonely, head to the nearest shopping mall to get out among other people.

622. Act as you imagine your hero would act.

623. Examine the many different steps that you could take to make your life better.

624. Turn on Martha Stewart's program to learn of interesting little ways to improve your home life.

625. Get a facial.

626. Go back to school for an advanced degree and lose yourself in your studies.

627. Stop in one of the new back rub salons for a minimassage during your lunch hour.

628. Glance through your morning newspaper to remind yourself that thousands of other people have problems too.

629. Make a new friend.

630. Take your vacation in the very near future.

631. Pat yourself on the back for doing as well as you have.

632. Weed your garden. Working outside will make you feel energized as well as in tune with nature.

633. Listen to birds singing their cheerful little tunes.

634. Read Norman Vincent Peale's wonderful books on positive thinking.

635. Get out a cassette tape of your favorite upbeat songs to play when you start to feel sad.

636. Make the most of moments spent waiting at appointments by reading self-help books.

637. Go see a stand-up comedian at a local comedy club.

638. Give yourself something to wear that makes you feel sexy again.

639. Make plans to visit a faraway friend or relative.

640. Attend your class reunion to surround yourself with all your old pals.

641. Build a snowman with an especially cheerful face. Nobody can frown while looking at a happy snowman.

642. Never allow your emotions to play tug-of-war with your plans for the day. Always take charge of your emotions and plan productive activities.

643. Stock your freezer full of gourmet TV dinners, so that you won't have to spend your energy fixing dinner on a particularly bad night.

644. Fill your office with lots of green plants.

645. Have breakfast in bed.

646. Talk to your significant other about your heartache.

647. People in pain tend to cut themselves off from friends. Don't fall into that pattern; you need your friends now more than ever.

648. When you are out of town on business, carry a photograph of your loved ones.

649. Work on becoming a billionaire.

650. Invite your friends over for a country tea party. The companionship and the tea will soothe your soul.

651. Have the best chef in town prepare your dinner. You deserve it!

652. Put your head down and just sob your heart out.

653. Wink—it will make you feel flirty and fun.

654. Get up early and go to bed late to help ensure a sound night's sleep.

655. Soak in a huge outdoor hot tub.

656. Find the dignity in your being.

657. Visit a sick friend. Your friend will feel better and you will too.

658. Dance the chicken dance. You can't look silly and feel sad at the same time.

659. Reserve the penthouse suite for the next time you travel out of town.

Disappointments are to the soul what a thunderstorm is to the air.

FRIEDRICH VON SCHILLER

660. Buck the status quo. Don't let others tell you how long your downtime will last. Just know that you'll be back in the happy lane in no time at all!

661. Volunteer at a food bank or kitchen.

662. Sing along with cheerful television and radio commercials.

663. Look great from head to toe.
Start off by getting a professional
shoe shine.

664. For the next hour pretend to be
someone else.

665. Consider joining the Peace Corps.

666. If you feel like wearing dark
clothing to express your mood,
make sure your clothes are still
stylish and flattering to you.

667. Celebrate having made it
through a tough week with a
bottle of Dom Pérignon champagne or a nonalcoholic wine.

668. Make an unexpected phone
call to a lost love.

669. Peel onions for a great excuse
to cry.

670. Think twice before making any huge confessions to friends.

671. Confide only when you feel that you must and reveal only what you need to share.

672. Head to the seashore.

673. Learn to improvise.

674. Sell your big, lonely house and move to a close-knit condo community.

675. Hold hands with your loved ones for support. Touch means so much!

676. Hum a cheery tune as you work around the house.

677. Open your drapes to let the sunshine into your home.

678. Hug your parents.

679. Go for a walk along the beach. Listen to the sounds of the surf and imagine your troubles being swept out to sea.

680. Reserve the best table at your favorite restaurant.

681. Attend a beautiful June wedding and get caught up in the atmosphere of romance.

682. Look for human-interest stories when you read the newspaper or a magazine.

683. Carve a big happy face in your morning toast to add a touch of whimsy to your day.

684. Refrain from calling psychic hot lines. Put down that phone!

685. Hug your children.

686. Call Dial-A-Joke for a little levity.

687. Imagine what the lives of those around you are really like. Your life might just be much better than you thought.

688. Visit an orchard during the summer and fall harvests to bring home bushels of healthy home-grown foods.

689. Get a roommate for company.

690. Move to an exciting city. How about New York, San Francisco, or Paris?

691. Contact the human resources department of your company about relocating.

692. Listen to a children's choir.

693. Plan a three-day weekend for yourself.

694. Send yourself a cheer-up card.

> *The Best Cheer-up Gifts Are:*
> *Extravagant*
> *Memorable*
> *Brightly colored*
> *Unexpected*
> *Beautifully gift wrapped*
> *Purchased with*
> *the receiver in mind*

695. Get an extra hour of sleep tonight.

696. Take an exciting world cruise.

697. Get tons of brochures on exotic vacation spots from your travel agent and enjoy the fantasy of visiting all of them.

698. Listen to the animal sounds of the late-night hours.

699. Believe that you have a guardian angel looking out for you at all times, even *now!*

700. Give yourself a nickname that captures your courageous spirit.

701. Watch a television talk show that deals with your particular situation.

702. Go through your address book and get in touch with old friends.

703. A great motto to live by is "If it is going to be, then it is up to me."

704. Find yourself a positive role model even if you're over eighty years of age. Everybody needs a mentor.

705. Learn CPR and maybe you can save a life!

706. Join a gourmet food club that sends a delicious treat each month, so you'll have something yummy to look forward to.

707. Marvel at the power of a summertime thunderstorm.

708. Splurge on something that you have always wanted for yourself.

709. Bake a batch of chocolate cupcakes and ice them with German chocolate topping. It is hard to find a more delicious treat.

710. Make a list of all your frustrations. Seeing them on paper will help you to form plans for solving them.

711. Take in a lost animal and give him a safe, wonderful home if you can't find his family. If you can, you'll make someone very happy.

712. Make the most of your talents and looks.

713. Ask your boss for advice if you have a personal relationship with her.

714. Read the Book of Proverbs for age-old wisdom.

715. Plant bulbs to bloom in the spring.

716. Dry flowers from bouquets that friends send to you, to remind yourself of their love.

717. Attend a self-discovery course.

718. Visit a monastery.

719. House-sit for a friend for a change of scenery.

720. Experience your second childhood.

721. To mark the middle of the week, celebrate Hump Day every Wednesday.

722. Change the order of the little things that you do each day.

723. Invent new reasons to celebrate.

724. Take a child to the park on a beautiful afternoon.

725. Move to one of the richest areas in the country:

   Marin County, California
   New York County, New York
   Westchester County, New York

   Who knows how your life might change for the better!

726. Make plans for Sweetest Day and Valentine's Day, so you won't have to be alone.

727. If you think your love life is a shambles, check out the troubles of Cathy in the comics.

728. Finish any project that you have started but haven't finished. This will give you a great feeling of accomplishment.

729. Sit down for a heart-to-heart chat with your favorite aunt.

730. Practice self-love by:
Caring for your health
Taking responsibility for your life
Respecting yourself

731. If your life has been really hectic lately, try a vacation at home instead of traveling somewhere. Your home will feel like a retreat.

732. Practice the Golden Rule: "Do unto others as you would have them do unto you."

733. Work toward loving all of yourself.

734. Grant yourself permission to be happy once again.

735. Bask in the love of your family and friends.

736. Pamper yourself from the time you get up in the morning till you go to bed at night.

737. Be like the armed forces—aim high!

738. Get rid of all the "what ifs" in your life.

739. Do you think that your problems are unusual? Did you know that there are even support groups for people like these:

  American Association of
   Dental Victims
  Messies Anonymous

740. Don't add to all the negativity in the world. Keep a positive attitude.

741. Understand that no man is an island, not even you!

742. Try to look at the world from a spiritual perspective.

743. Know that for having loved and lost, you are a richer person.

744. Strive to find a balance in your times of:
    Rest
    Work
    Play

745. If you feel that you have too much quiet time in your life, take a trip to a busy, crowded city.

746. Stop idealizing the future compared to the present.

747. Understand that your attitude makes a huge difference in at least 95 percent of your life.

748. If you can't be happy today, at least be satisfied with the way you are choosing to live your life.

749. The best way to view your troubles is from the vantage point of a bowed head and bended knee.

Create Your Own
Secret Hideaway That Includes:
Soft lighting
A rocking chair
Flowers
Plants
Music
Great books
Prayer books
A quilt to wrap up in

750. Keep in mind that your life doesn't have to be perfect for you to be happy.

751. Realize that once you get past poverty, money does not buy happiness.

752. Trust your own unique point of view.

753. It is a spiritual law that what you resist sticks, so don't fight your bad mood. Learn to transcend it.

754. Understand that research shows that actively religious people recover faster from hurts than nonreligious people do.

755. Keep in mind that inactivity breeds emotional troubles.

756. Stay busy. Happiness is a side effect of doing other things.

757. Maintain your close personal relationships—they will help you to recover faster.

758. Feeling cooped up? Rent Alfred Hitchcock's *Rear Window* for some commiseration.

759. Eat an apple a day to keep the doctor away. (Stress lowers your resistance to illness, so eat healthy.)

760. Learn to have a hero's heart.

761. You can change. Set your mind to it.

762. Buy a CD of whale songs and play it on a mighty sound system.

763. Stop picking on yourself. You wouldn't pick on a friend, so don't put yourself down.

764. One of the best things you can do for another human being is to listen to his point of view. Start listening.

765. Develop your sense of empathy for others' troubles.

766. Learn the art of staying calm during an emotional storm.

767. Are you feeling as if you are the only person who is alone? Not true! Three times as many people live alone now as did fifty years ago.

768. Tonight when you set the table for dinner, use cheerful kids' china.

769. Learn to accept blame, however painful this might be for you.

770. Find your place in the world.

771. Read the wonderful fable of the ant and the dove, which tells that a good deed is always repaid.

772. Do unusual activities, just for the fun of them.

773. Take your own advice.

774. Think you have troubles? Read Kelsey Grammer's autobiography.

775. Take it easy on yourself.

776. Work to have harmony among your mind, body, and soul.

777. If you are going in one direction and it isn't working, make a turn. Keep turning till you find the right path for you.

778. Read the writings of Ralph Waldo Emerson for inspiration.

779. Hire a personal trainer.

780. Try to meet your office deadlines.

781. If you have a vacation coming up and want to stay busy, try a working vacation such as building houses with Habitat for Humanity.

782. Pick a personality trait that you would like to see more of in your personality. Try:
    Tolerance
    Strength
    Patience

783. When you make plans with
friends, be sure to keep them,
no matter how tempted you are
to break them because you
aren't in a happy frame of mind.

784. Visit with your neighbor's dog.

785. Give yourself a break.
Another one.
And another one!
Get the point?

786. Refrain from being rude. That
includes not just making remarks
but not cutting other drivers off
in traffic, not pushing into line,
and the like.

787. Buy a lottery ticket. You can at
least look forward to the draw-
ing, and yes, a cool million might
be just the thing to ease the pain
of your broken heart.

788. Join a crusade to help the homeless.

789. Spend an hour reading your favorite magazine from cover to cover.

790. Just grin and bear it till things get better.

791. Kick up your heels.

792. Sing yourself a happy lullaby before you drift off to sleep.

793. Never add insult to injury.

794. Use your willpower to force yourself to keep on trying.

795. Be open to others' suggestions.

796. Yes, sometimes the truth hurts. Just be brave and take it like a soldier.

797. Search for unusual ways to cheer yourself up.

798. Give yourself a little pep talk on the way to work.

799. Write a letter to your favorite celebrity and request an autographed photo.

800. Start the healing process from right where you are *now!*

801. Spread all the good news that you can.

802. Never turn back when times get hard.

803. Face your fears, and then they will disappear.

804. If you must, go out on a limb. Isn't that where the fruit is anyway?

Life is hard by the yard;
But by the inch, life's a cinch.

AUTHOR UNKNOWN

805. Don't take the simple things in life for granted.

806. Buy a box of sixty-four Crayola crayons and a new coloring book, and pretend to be a six-year old.

807. Love everybody!

808. Go out of your way to be helpful to others.

809. Make a ten-foot-tall snowman after the next big snowfall.

810. Show compassion to those who need it.

811. Follow what your gut instinct tells you to do.

812. Remember, "To thine own heart be true."

813. Know that you will cheer up faster if you are an openhearted person.

814. Develop a love of learning.

815. Spend part of every serious conversation you have listening to other people talk about their troubles.

816. Develop a quest for the truth.

817. Climb up to a tree house and look out at the world through your inner child's eyes. Innocence can be a very enlightening experience.

818. Take a nature walk to clear your head.

819. Have a soda at a quaint and friendly neighborhood bar.

820. Share a roll of Life Savers with someone else who is down in the dumps.

821. Take a catamaran ride on a pretty day.

822. Spend an evening browsing through mail-order catalogs and magazines learning the latest fashion trends, so that you can plan a whole new look for yourself.

823. For a change of pace, go on a wintertime picnic that includes hot chocolate, homemade cookies, a heavy blanket, candles, and soft music.

824. Cut fresh flowers from your garden and brighten up your workplace with them.

825. Prepare an Easter basket made up of all your childhood favorites and take it to your office to share with your work pals.

826. Count your blessings one by one.

827. Even when you are home alone for dinner, get out your fine china and silver to create a pretty place setting.

828. Sit on a park bench and people-watch. You will soon begin to notice that lots of people look as if they have a broken heart.

829. Get involved in a card club that meets on a regular basis, to have a mindless activity to fill up some lonely hours.

830. Create your own homepage on the World Wide Web.

Here are some telephone numbers that you might find helpful:

National Mental Health Association
800-969-6642

National Runaway Switchboard
800-621-4000

Childhelp's National Child Abuse Hotline
800-422-4453

National AIDS Hotline
800-342-AIDS

National Hospice Organization
703-243-5900

American Suicide Foundation
800-531-4477

831. Take a bike ride around a local college campus and enjoy all the youthful energy in the air.

832. Browse through Saks Fifth Avenue and dream of all the things you are going to buy yourself after you make it through this rough period of your life.

833. Tell a child a bedtime story.

834. Start a new project that won't feel overwhelming but is large enough to take up a considerable amount of your time. For example, make a new bed for your furry pet friend or build him a new house.

835. Make a quick escape—go to sleep.

836. Get up early, and spend at least half an hour exercising.

837. Learn to cook one fabulous gourmet meal so that you can invite company over for dinner and serve them in style.

838. If you have trouble sleeping, ask your doctor for a sleeping aid.

839. Buy a fun, silly pillowcase for your pillow.

840. Watch reruns of your favorite comedy.

841. When it rains, carry a wild umbrella and wear a brightly colored raincoat.

842. Visit a local bakery and indulge your sweet tooth with all of your favorite pastries.

843. Look through an old scrapbook and remember all your happier times.

844. Spend a lonely Saturday at the office catching up on all your work.

845. Sit on a porch swing chatting with loved ones.

846. Spend the night at a beautiful country inn where you'll have privacy and be pampered.

847. Treat yourself to a wonderful Mont Blanc pen to write in your diary with.

848. Keep busy, even if you have to make up silly things to keep yourself occupied.

849. Stay up late to watch the fire die and to plan for all your tomorrows.

850. Sit by a campfire and share stories with your childhood friends.

One must be fond of people and trust them if one is not to make a mess of life.

E. M. FORSTER

851. Put a nice portion of your salary into savings to ensure a happy ending to your rainy days.

852. Shovel an elderly neighbor's driveway after a big storm—it will make you feel really good about yourself.

853. Throw out any clothes that don't make you feel good.

854. Stop to buy fresh flowers for yourself from a street vendor.

855. Make someone else's day by leaving a huge tip the next time you receive great service at a restaurant.

856. Embrace each change of the seasons and know that your life will change too.

857. Paint your bedroom passion pink.

858. Play with your favorite child-hood toys.

859. Sleep with your favorite child-hood stuffed animal.

860. Take your dog for a long walk in the woods.

861. Feel like staying under the covers and never facing the world? Then treat yourself to a beautiful Dior nightie for your period of hibernation.

862. Have a summertime romance.

863. Lounge by the pool all
    weekend.

864. Spend a little time at a children's
    museum.

865. Read the Scriptures every night
    before falling to sleep.

866. Attend a large cocktail party
    and get lost in all the mindless
    small talk.

867. View a lighthouse at night. It is
    good to see a light in the dark.

868. Make a wish list.

869. Take up marathon running.
    Running long distances gives
    you a lot of time to sort things
    out in your mind.

870. Instead of staying in this evening,
     go out for a few hours.

871. Sip a glass of eggnog by a beau-
     tifully decorated Christmas tree.

872. Go see the latest block-
     buster movie.

873. Wear a pretty spring hat to lift
     your spirits.

874. Give yourself a piece of dia-
     mond jewelry.

875. Be childlike and take a trip to
     Disneyland or Disney World.

876. Browse a toy store to feel like a
     kid again. A recommendation:
     the nearest F. A. O. Schwarz.

877. Nibble on chocolate chip
     cookie dough.

878. Get yourself some tropical fish to watch during stressful moments. You will find them very relaxing.

879. Read the best-seller *Dogs Never Lie About Love* by Jeffrey Moussaieff Masson. It will warm your heart.

880. Tour a mansion and imagine what it would be like if you lived there.

881. Take good care of all the little ones affected by your troubles.

882. Work to maintain a stable lifestyle.

883. Try to understand that you are the only person in the world who can make you feel any emotion at all. Therefore, choose to feel only healthy emotions.

884. Give your heart a little workout of a nonemotional kind. Take some risks to get your heart pumping and your mind off your worries. Try:

    A roller-coaster ride
    White-water rafting
    Parasailing
    Skydiving

885. What do you love to do? Okay, stop putting it off and plan to do it today!

886. Take the road less traveled.

887. Stay clear of people who will bring you down.

888. Stay clear of problems that will bring you down.

889. Take a little nap after dinner.

890. Start a training program for your mind to learn to think in positive and healing kinds of ways.

891. If you have tons of anger, get some professional help to work through it.

892. Read a gothic romance.

893. Blow bubbles with your bubble gum.

894. Keep in mind that today is the only day that you really have.

895. Smile, wink, and kick up your feet!

896. Be sincere.

897. Realize that, in the end, love does conquer all.

*It is difficult to make a man
miserable while he feels
that he is worthy of himself
and claims kindred to
the great God who made him.*

ABRAHAM LINCOLN

898. Get rid of the boredom factor in your life.

899. Silently say the word "love" whenever you come into contact with another human being who is causing you some stress.

900. Keep in mind that who you are inside is much greater than you ever imagined and that you are capable of rising above this difficulty in life.

901. In the summertime, prepare yummy desserts for yourself from fresh berries. Especially recommended: strawberry shortcake or blackberry cobbler.

902. For a quick escape, go jogging.

903. Make a list of all your friends, and then beside each name write down a way that each person could help you. Now call each friend and ask for their help.

904. Go to a mountaintop resort and contemplate your next step.

905. Teach an old dog a new trick, and then maybe you'll understand that you can learn a new trick or two yourself.

906. Make a wish when you see a new moon.

907. Take up photography, and take pictures of all your blessings.

908. Swim, surf, or water-ski—anything to get you out and having fun in the sun.

909. Listen to a sad song and cry to release your emotions.

910. Read a book on astronomy to grasp how big the universe really is and how insignificant your troubles really are.

911. Stroll over to the nearest designer boutique and buy yourself a fabulous outfit.

912. Have a champagne toast with breakfast tomorrow.

913. If you want to feel good about yourself, just do something good.

914. Throw on your favorite baseball cap and head to the park for an impromptu game of catch with some of the neighborhood kids.

915. To warm up on the outside and on the inside, have a big bowl of homemade vegetable soup on a cold winter's night.

916. Become the spark in your lover's fire.

917. Build a huge sand castle and then watch it fall into the ocean. Imagine that your troubles are crumbling just like the sand castle.

918. Realize that there are no such things as coincidences.

919. Take high tea in an elegant hotel.

920. Hire a landscape architect to beautifully landscape your yard, to give you pleasure on weekends, and to give your eyes a treat when you return home each evening.

921. Put these attitudes to work in your life:
     Giving
     Loving
     Sharing

922. Get your hair cut really short. You will feel younger and perkier.

923. Sit in an old rocker on the front porch and let yourself have a really long cry.

924. Wander through an antiques store and see how times have changed. Know that your life will change in time too.

925. Spend time at a library reading up on current solutions to your problems.

926. Be the kind of friend who always lends a helping hand.

927. Plan a grocery store buying spree of fun, outrageous junk food.

928. Play your favorite sad country songs on a jukebox.

929. Visit with your grandparents and ask for their wise counsel.

930. Wear a bright ribbon in your hair.

931. Place a window box outside your bedroom window, so you'll wake up to a very pretty view every morning.

932. Listen to the wonderful sound of wind chimes in the early-morning breeze.

933. Play music from your high school years.

934. Swing on a tire hung from a tree limb.

935. Order a nice big, juicy steak with all the trimmings for dinner.

936. Play hooky from a chore you have been meaning to do.

937. For a diversion, learn a new job skill.

938. Indulge your sweet tooth with an ice-cream pie.

939. Rent a convertible for a beautiful day of exploring your hometown.

940. Read through your old diaries to remember your happier times.

941. At lunch, find a corner table in a quaint café and enjoy the atmosphere.

*To Become
Young-hearted Again, Try:*

*Collecting dolls
Building model trains
Finger painting
Roller-skating
Playing games
Bicycling*

942. Look at your wedding photographs to see your brightest smile. Know that you will one day see that smile again.

943. Listen to motivational tapes in the morning while you dress.

944. Read through some really old newspapers to see how times have changed during just your lifetime.

945. Go out today and purchase two or three books on how to deal with stress. Start reading them tonight.

946. Purchase the latest issues of all your favorite magazines that have articles that deal with your kind of troubles.

947. During the wintertime, start your own greenhouse.

948. After a particularly hard day, plop into your favorite armchair and just daydream your heart out.

949. Order room service when you are out of town on business.

950. In a lonely hotel room, pick up and read the Bible.

951. Look for serendipitous events, to see how God is working things out for you.

952. Remember not to take life too seriously. After all, you will never get out of it alive!

953. Go horseback riding for a feeling of power and freedom.

954. Give the gift of life—blood. You will feel as if you are making a big difference, and you are.

955. Check out the great view from a high-rise building and consider getting an uptown apartment.

956. Play soft chamber music as a soothing background noise to keep you company.

957. Read your morning newspaper at a park, or at least on your patio.

958. Enroll in a flower-arranging class to develop a new talent and to make your home a little brighter.

959. Plant a tree; at least the environment will be happy.

960. Get your mind off yourself by tutoring a child.

961. Rent an oceanfront condo for a wonderful change of scenery.

962. Become a nature lover.

963. Organize a neighborhood picnic.

964. Teach an adult to read.

965. To spice up your life, cook with unusual herbs and spices.

966. Learn to say no to unreasonable requests for your time.

967. Visit your loved ones' graves.

968. Set up a lunch date this week with your mentor.

969. Surprise a good friend with a gift for no special occasion.

970. Take a day trip to a fun nearby city.

971. Whenever you visit the zoo, be sure to stop by the monkey cages.

972. Buy a juicer and start off your mornings with delicious and healthy fruit concoctions.

973. Create a little beauty in your community by joining the Adopt-a-Spot programs.

974. Remember your childhood dreams. Maybe it's not too late to start living them.

Many men owe the grandeur of their lives to their tremendous difficulties.

C. H. SPURGEON

975. The next time you spot a butterfly, imagine that your troubles are flying away on its beautiful wings.

976. Remember that life usually offers lots of options for most problems.

977. Keep in mind that troubles shared are often cut in half.

978. Get this—bad things happen in everybody's life, not just yours.

979. Listen to your conscience. It was put there for a reason.

980. Pursue job opportunities that allow you to challenge yourself.

981. Look for your healing to come from within, not from the outside.

982. Move to a foreign country for a year.

983. Go after all the things you want from every area of your life.

984. Head to the sunshine states for a long-overdue rest:
    Florida
    Arizona
    Hawaii
    California

985. You build muscles by picking up heavy objects. Think how strong your heart will be from carrying this heavy load.

986. No night lasts forever. Your dark-
ness will end too!

987. Doubt your doubts, never
your beliefs.

988. Know that the past is over and it
can't be changed, but the
future can be altered.

989. Read the poetry of Helen Steiner
Rice for a real spirit booster.

990. Start your own business.

991. Rent the movie *Scrooge,* even if
it isn't Christmastime.

992. Vow to earn a million dollars during the next twelve months.

993. Reconcile with an estranged
family member or friend.

994. Know that only by going through rough times can you find your inner resources, which you never knew you had before heartache struck your world.

995. Ask your friends not to gossip about your troubles.

996. Marvel at how wonderfully your body works.

997. Wave to a plane and imagine your blues flying away on its wings.

998. Contemplate the true meaning of life.

999. Read the marvelous book *The Precious Present,* by Spencer Johnson.

1,000. Say "Good morning" to God every day.

1,001. Rid yourself of any resentment that you may be feeling toward others.

1,002. Track down your closest child-hood friend. The renewal of that special bond will be good for your heart.

1,003. Substitute juice, tea, coffee, soft drinks, or other nonalcoholic beverages for cocktails.

1,004. Some researchers believe that foods high in selenium may relieve depression. You might want to try nibbling on sunflower seeds to test their theory.

1,005. Believe it or not, some folks even use red onions to help induce sleep. So, when you can't sleep, fix an onion dip for a late-night snack.

1,006. Read the timeless wisdom of Winnie-the-Pooh.

Laugh a little, sing a little
As you go your way!
Work a little, play a little
Do this every day!

Give a little, take a little,
Never mind a frown,
Make your smile a welcomed thing
All around the town.

Laugh a little, love a little,
Skies are always blue!
Every cloud has silver linings,
But it's up to you!

AUTHOR UNKNOWN

1,007. When you feel uptight, try doing a few shoulder shrugs. Simply lift your shoulders as high as you can and then release them.

1,008. Try to relieve your tension by doing head rolls. Just drop your head forward to your chest and then rotate it around your body. Repeat several times.

1,009. If you decide to drink an alcoholic beverage with dinner, limit it to one glass.

1,010. To help you relax, get a CD of environmental sounds.

1,011. Go from head to toe relaxing each of the muscles throughout your body. If you will do this exercise slowly, you will feel much better immediately.

1,012. Lift your spirits by trying a natural remedy known to elevate one's mood, such as St. John's wort.

1,013. Give up the notion that life is fair.

1,014. Learn a new job skill.

1,015. People have common stress points in their lives:

    Change   Fear
    Heartache Grief
    Inactivity

1,016. The secret of success is learning how to use your troubles and learn from them.

1,017. Keep in mind that everyone suffers from major life trials at one time or another. You are not unusual!

1,018. Understand that you will feel less stressed when you can take charge of a situation, instead of taking a passive role.

1,019. Give up the emotion of apathy. Get involved with life!

1,020. Get healthy! You will be able to heal faster from a broken heart if you are in good health.

1,021. Take up a serious study of philosophy.

1,022. Keep your expectations about your holidays in check. Be realistic.

1,023. Condition yourself to seek fulfill-ment in healthy choices.

1,024. Get this: You have to cheer up or you might start experiencing these stress-related illnesses:

Asthma
Migraines
Digestive problems
Heartburn
Skin upsets

Don't you think this is reason enough to get busy and do your healing work?

1,025. You need to have a restful home environment. If you feel that your space is too crowded, your neighbors too noisy, or that your stuff is taking over your life, consider moving to a new place.

1,026. Give yourself a little rest period during your workday.

1,027. Every single day, be sure to do some activities that require a degree of physical exertion.

1,028. Give up smoking. A healthy heart is a happy heart.

1,029. Try to eat slowly and enjoy your evening meal, even if you are eating alone.

1,030. Take heed—type A personalities suffer more from stress-related problems due to a broken heart.

1,031. Always vent your anger in constructive, not destructive, ways.

1,032. Need professional help?
Here's how to find a qualified
therapist:

Consult your family doctor
Call your local mental-health
agency
Ask friends for referrals
Check with your minister
Visit your company
psychiatrist

1,033. Remind yourself that you are
never alone, for God is always
with you.

1,034. Don't close yourself off
from others.

1,035. Surround yourself with friends
who make you feel safe, loved,
and comfortable.

1,036. Don't rely on drugs or alcohol to help you make it through lonely nights.

The optimist is as often wrong as the pessimist, but he is far happier.

AUTHOR UNKNOWN

1,037. Forgive yourself for all the mistakes that have led you to this point in your life.

1,038. Try to express any positive feelings that you have, no matter how trivial they seem. The more joy you give out, the more joy you will get back.

1,039. Keep your ears and eyes open to hear the lessons you need to learn at this point in your life.

1,040. Know that one is not a lonely number. It is just a number.

1,041. If you see a therapist, be honest with her, as well as yourself.

1,042. Give yourself something to celebrate, such as:

> Arbor Day
> Children's Day
> Citizenship Day
> Election Day
> Fellowship Day
> Poetry Day
> Loyalty Day
> Old Maid's Day
> Groundhog Day
> National Day of Prayer

1,043. Slow down. Stop pushing yourself so much.

1,044. Work on your fears. Don't give in to them.

1,045. Plan each moment of the day to do what feels right to you.

1,046. Watch a television church service.

1,047. Write a letter of apology to anyone you have wronged.

1,048. Compliment yourself. After all, you know your best qualities.

1,049. Whatever you want others to give you, be sure to give it to yourself first.

1,050. Know that spring always follows winter.

1,051. Talk a lot. You need to express your feelings. If you must, talk to yourself.

1,052. Listen to and learn from others who have been in your shoes.

1,053. Accept the consequences of any mistakes that you have made.

1,054. Don't sweat the little stuff.

1,055. Know that tomorrow will come no matter what you try to do to stop it.

1,056. Think of all the heroines and heroes you have read about and imagine how they would react if they were in your shoes. Try thinking like:

Connecticut Yankee
Huckleberry Finn
Camille
Scrooge
Ali Baba
Perry Mason
Jane Eyre
Robinson Crusoe

1,057. Ask yourself if you are getting any emotional payoffs from holding on to your pain.

1,058. Look at the *big* picture.

1,059. Lighten up on those closest to you.

1,060. Every single day, learn a new way to cheer yourself up.

1,061. If others are also affected by the cause of your heartache, be careful not to let them bring you down.

1,062. Set a goal to meet three new people in the next two weeks.

1,063. It is always darkest before the dawn. Watch for the first rays of hope!

1,064. Misery loves company, so be careful.

1,065. If you do the same thing, you'll get the same results. So, if you want to feel better, make a change.

1,066. Track down a college professor who had a huge influence on your life and have a heart-to-heart talk.

1,067. Celebrate Friday the thirteenth instead of thinking that it will bring you even more bad luck.

1,068. Keep in mind that a life shared is twice blessed!

1,069. Wear glamorous silk pj's when you are lounging around the house, to feel like a movie star.

1,070. When you are feeling your most vulnerable, stick with the familiar.

1,071. Keep in mind that other people have the same problems that you have. Look for the many different ways people deal with them.

1,072. Say good night to God each night before you go to sleep.

1,073. Are you having a hard time during the Christmas holidays? Read *A Cup of Christmas Tea,* by Tom Hegg, to lift your spirits.

1,074. Call your favorite cousin for a long-overdue chitchat.

1,075. Firmly believe that you can get through everything that you need to face.

1,076. To cheer yourself up when you have a little boo-boo, wear a colored Band-Aid.

1,077. Everyone needs someone; don't try to make it alone.

> *The diamond cannot*
> *be polished without friction,*
> *nor man perfected*
> *without trials.*
> AUTHOR UNKNOWN

1,078. You have a vital role to play in the universe. Get busy!

1,079. Start spending more time alone as you feel stronger.

1,080. Take a small step in the direction of your dreams.

1,081. Take a walk in the fog and just lose your troubles in the mist.

1,082. Do something every day to prove to yourself that you love you.

1,083. Join a support group at your church.

1,084. Send out good thoughts to everyone around you.

1,085. Attend a midnight mass.

1,086. Realize that there are millions of people in other parts of the world who would gladly change places with you.

1,087. Take a risk that will allow you to prove to yourself that you are stronger and braver than you ever imagined.

1,088. Spend the night outside under the stars.

1,089. Watch the waves crash to shore and get lost in the sound and motion of the scene.

1,090. If you think you have problems, listen to the latest political scandal.

1,091. Act like a child for an entire day.

1,092. Ask a friend to help you practice positive self-talk.

1,093. Listen to the happy sounds of the holidays:

> Firecrackers and fireworks on
> the Fourth of July
> Christmas music
> Thanksgiving gatherings
> Children hunting for Easter eggs
> Kids bobbing for apples at
> Halloween
> Romantic songs playing on
> Valentine's Day

1,094. Bake yourself a wonderful fruit pie and enjoy the fabulous aroma.

1,095. Believe that all the compliments you receive are true.

1,096. Buy all new cosmetics in the latest, hottest colors to enhance your appearance.

The Most Common
Causes of Sadness:

Death of a loved one
Divorce
Major illness
Getting fired from a job
Retirement
Moving
Losing a friend
Financial difficulties
Losing a pet
Romantic breakup

1,097. Make a detailed list of all the options you have at this point in your life.

1,098. Become the guardian of a sweet and beautiful Bernese mountain dog.

1,099. Do a favor for your boss, and it might just improve your work situation.

1,100. Make a homemade greeting card for the friend who has helped you the most.

1,101. Order a huge L. L. Bean dog bed for your "baby," so that he can get a good night's sleep after taking care of you and your troubles all day long.

1,102. Ask your grandmother to fix your favorite recipe from your childhood.

1,103. Be frugal for the next few months till you get your feet back on solid ground.

1,104. Throw out all your junk mail, unopened. You have more important things to do with your time.

1,105. Too many phone calls getting you tense? Get an unlisted number.

1,106. Associate with upbeat, positive people, even if it means making new friends.

1,107. Surrender to your emotions in private or only with close friends and family members.

1,108. Order one of everything from the dessert cart at a French restaurant.

1,109. Attend a hog-calling contest. You might feel crazy, but you won't feel sad.

1,110. Fall in love with your spouse all over again.

1,111. Whenever you have a heart-to-heart talk, do it face-to-face.

1,112. Try to make friends everywhere you go, to help you feel less alone in this big world.

1,113. Reach out to everyone around you, even if only by saying hello each morning to your coworkers and neighbors.

1,114. Create a neighborhood watch group, so that you will feel safer.

1,115. Read *A Christmas Carol,* by Charles Dickens.

1,116. Get into the holiday spirit by going Christmas shopping in New York, Chicago, or any really large, exciting city.

1,117. Experience springtime in Paris.

1,118. Make a cow (and your heart) happy by giving up eating red meat.

1,119. When you feel your worst, wear your finest.

1,120. Embrace all the remaining good in your life.

1,121. Buy a great new sweater to wear on cold nights when you feel lonely.

1,122. Plan an "accidental" meeting with someone who can help you.

1,123. Get one of your heartfelt poems published.

1,124. Read one of your poems at a trendy little coffeehouse.

1,125. Dine under the stars.

1,126. When you go to get a puppy, treat yourself to the pick of the litter.

1,127. Attend a major dog show. After all, who could feel sad when surrounded by tons of hearts wrapped in fur?

1,128. Start your morning with cinnamon rolls baking in the oven and freshly brewed coffee.

1,129. Have a French picnic with a loaf of French bread, cheese, and a bottle of fine wine.

1,130. Help someone to find a lost pet.

1,131. On a Sunday afternoon, go for an old-fashioned drive in the country.

1,132. Make a childhood feast of sugar bread and chocolate milk.

1,133. With every problem in your life, you can decide to become either bitter or better. Choose to become better.

1,134. If you want a different perspective on life, go to a foreign film
festival.

1,135. Head to the best delicatessen in
town and order the biggest sand-
wich on the menu. Go hog-wild.

1,136. Keep a tin of gourmet cookies
under your bed for the nights
when you can't sleep.

1,137. After a big Sunday dinner, take a
long stroll with someone you
care about.

1,138. Dress according to the weather
predictions, so that you don't
get sick.

1,139. When it's late at night and you
can't sleep, get up and walk
around instead of lying in bed
and dwelling on your troubles.

How to Meditate:
Find a quiet place
Sit upright
Close your eyes
Relax your body
from feet to head
Picture a lovely scene
Concentrate on a meaningful word
Reject all distracting thoughts
Stay at it for fifteen
to twenty minutes
Open your eyes and relax

1,140. Read the Bible cover to cover.

1,141. Memorize Scripture passages that pertain to your particular situation.

1,142. Make the most of every day of your life, even the painful ones.

1,143. When you dine out, sit at a table by a window and watch the world go by.

The tragedy of life is not so much what men suffer, but rather what they miss.

Thomas Carlyle

1,144. This Easter, buy a huge, floppy Easter bonnet to hide your sad smile.

1,145. Write to Ann Landers for her take on your situation.

1,146. Hang out at a blues bar.

1,147. View a meteor shower and get caught up in the wonder of it all.

1,148. Lie on your back and watch cloud formations. What are you picturing?

1,149. Play upbeat songs on the instrument you played as a child.

1,150. Paint your home interior in a bright, cheery shade of yellow.

1,151. Drink your first cup of coffee for the day from a mug with a cheerful motto on it.

1,152. For a happy daydream, remember:

Your first kiss
Your first car
A big surprise party
Receiving an award
A childhood dance
The first day of summer
  vacation

1,153. Browse through a charming country store.

1,154. At your workplace, cut yourself off from needless office gossip.

1,155. Get a new set of cheerful dishes to dine on when you eat alone.

1,156. Help a child, and treat your sweet tooth at the same time, by purchasing a box of Girl Scout cookies.

1,157. Talk baby talk to your pet. You'll feel silly—and you can't feel silly and be sad at the same time.

1,158. Write thank-you notes to all the people who have helped you in the last month.

1,159. Participate in an Earth Day celebration to get a sense of being involved with Mother Nature.

1,160. Try to see eye to eye with your loved ones.

1,161. Join the YMCA or the YWCA.

1,162. Share a rope of licorice candy with someone you find exciting.

1,163. On a pretty day, head to the park for a good workout with your furry friend.

1,164. Carry a funny good-luck charm.

1,165. Plan your wardrobe carefully. Get all your clothes in great shape through dry cleaning and alterations. If you look good, you'll feel good.

1,166. Look in your attic for mementos that hold special meaning for you.

1,167. Buy fun-colored Hush Puppies or Keds. You will feel like a kid again!

1,168. Host a family reunion. It will mean so much to be around your loved ones at this point in your life.

1,169. Make your next vacation a quiet, relaxing one.

1,170. Blow bubble-gum bubbles.

1,171. Host a power lunch at a childlike restaurant.

1,172. Do you need to lower your blood pressure? Pet your dog for fifteen minutes a day; it has been proven to lower one's blood pressure.

1,173. Treat yourself to a weekend at a five-star resort.

1,174. Get out your headset and listen to constructive self-help tapes while you do your yard work.

1,175. Leave tomorrow until it arrives.

1,176. The only speed to set your life by is Godspeed.

1,177. When you buy yourself something that you have really been wanting for a long time, have it beautifully gift-wrapped.

1,178. Avoid eating too many chocolates if caffeine bothers you.

1,179. Consider the use of hypnotherapy to help heal your broken heart.

1,180. Mend a broken friendship.

1,181. Get your happiness from the things you can see only with your heart.

1,182. Do you have deep, dark secrets? Tell them to only a time-tested, trusted confidant.

1,183. Give up saying "never again" to trying again.

1,184. Do your best when it matters most. The rest of the time, give yourself a break.

1,185. Stop indulging yourself with bad moods.

1,186. Pay cash, as you don't need any financial troubles.

1,187. Stop viewing yourself as someone on a downhill skid.

1,188. Do the ordinary stuff in an extraordinary way.

1,189. Accomplish something from your *emotional* "To Do" list.

1,190. Test-drive expensive cars.

1,191. Learn the art of detachment.

1,192. Fight injustice.

1,193. Keep all your promises, especially those made to yourself.

1,194. Don't punish those who have hurt you.

1,195. Put the power of laughter to work for you.

1,196. Find the joy and beauty in nature.

1,197. Rent an animal movie, such as:

> *Benji*
> *101 Dalmatians*
> *Lady and the Tramp*
> *Homeward Bound*
> *Old Yeller*

1,198. Give up seeing yourself as a victim of certain circumstances.

1,199. Join a spiritual book club to soothe your tired soul.

1,200. Fill your mind with powerful, healing thoughts.

1,201. Imagine yourself being in your friend's, boss's, lover's shoes. Would you be any happier?

1,202. If you must make a major decision, allow yourself plenty of time to make a wise one.

1,203. When trying to heal your bad mood, think creatively.

> *He who fears he will suffer,*
> *already suffers*
> *because of his fear.*
>
> MICHEL DE MONTAIGNE

1,204. Always tell the truth. Your conscience needs to be clear for your soul to soar.

1,205. If you feel lonely, run over to a neighbor's house for a quick visit.

1,206. Look at the causes of your gloomy mood from at least ten different angles.

1,207. Never allow your bad mood to stop you or hold you back.

1,208. Strive to reach the dawn.

1,209. Browse through bookstores looking for books that will keep your mind occupied till the wee small hours of the morning.

1,210. If you feel like pointing a finger, turn it toward yourself. After all, change starts there.

1,211. Before you face the little traumas in your day-to-day life, take three short breaths.

1,212. Never hang your head in defeat.

1,213. Practice KISS: Keep it simple, silly.

1,214. Put a sign on your door that says GONE FISHIN' when you need to get in touch with your feelings.

1,215. If you believe that something in the world needs to be changed in order to prevent others from falling victim to your circumstances, make the necessary changes to help them.

1,216. Take up a new hobby, such as:

Pasta making	Bird-watching
Quilting	Backpacking
Juggling	Gardening
Fishing	Boccie
Canoeing	Bonsai
Antiquing	Canning
Horseback riding	Beekeeping

1,217. Join your church choir.

1,218. Never sulk!

1,219. Take scenic detours from time to time.

1,220. Indulge your sweet tooth with:

Bonbons	Caramels
Divinity	Fudge
Penuche	Pralines
Jelly beans	Malted milk balls

Or try some of your own child-hood favorites!

1,221. Live your life by your rules, not your parents' or your siblings', and not your spouse's.

1,222. Buy a couple of prayer books, and put them to good use.

1,223. Plan a party so you'll have something fun to look forward to in the near future.

1,224. Having cold feet about the future? Buy some rag-wool socks to keep your toes nice and toasty.

1,225. Give up coveting what you've lost that others around you still have.

1,226. Before you go to bed tonight, try to settle any differences that you have with your loved ones.

1,227. Try really, really hard to get excited about your life again.

1,228. Redesign your life.

1,229. View problems as challenges.

1,230. See troubles as opportunities.

1,231. Trust your own point of view.

1,232. Visit a shrine. How about:
Shrine of the Holy Shroud—
Turin, Italy
Lincoln Memorial—
Washington, D.C.
Ste. Anne de Beaupré—
Quebec, Canada
Tomb of the Unknowns—
Arlington, Virginia
Taj Mahal—Agra, India

1,233. Be sensible; keep your emotions in check.

1,234. Help plan a wedding, shower, or any other happy event.

1,235. Let your actions speak of peace, love, and healing.

1,236. Be proud of your uniqueness.

1,237. Attend a stress management clinic.

1,238. Understand that forcing yourself to get moving will give you more energy.

1,239. Spend time in activities that make you into a better person.

How to Cheer Up Your Spouse:
Ask what you can do
Be available
Show your love
Give emotional support
Make cheering her up
a top priority

1,240. Give yourself a little shock: Take a chilly moonlit swim.

1,241. Shake hands with a famous person.

1,242. Ask yourself what you could be doing differently that would help to cheer you up. Then do it.

1,243. Spend time with people who appreciate you.

1,244. Work for a company that acknowledges your worth to it.

1,245. If it comes down to being right or being happy, choose being happy.

1,246. Keep in mind that the world has seen problems much larger than yours.

1,247. Go against the grain. Dare to be different.

1,248. Realize that life is a journey, not a destination.

1,249. Head over to the nearest coffeehouse and have a wonderful cup of java.

1,250. Join a club.

1,251. Take a snuggle break with your significant other or with your furry friend.

1,252. Break your big goals down into workable little ones.

1,253. Work on ways to expand your self-esteem.

1,254. Try holistic approaches to solving your problems.

1,255. To help rid your mind of negatives, try healing through the use of literature. Expand your mind and perspectives through a well-thought-out program of reading.

1,256. Take a horse-drawn carriage ride early in the morning, when the world is just waking up.

1,257. Become a you pleaser, not a people pleaser.

1,258. Consider trying brain expansion work, whereby you develop both sides of your brain to make you a more well-rounded person.

1,259. Are you crushed because you haven't reached a goal in your life? Try again. Persistence pays off.

1,260. Have you tried too many times to reach a certain goal but can't? Then set new goals for yourself.

1,261. Try Holotropic Breathwork, which promotes healing and expansion through deep breathing and music.

1,262. Allow yourself the luxury of working through your emotional baggage and not just pushing it under the rug.

1,263. Take a wild and crazy ride on a roller coaster, and your troubles will be the last thing on your mind.

1,264. Vow to live so that from now on you don't have regrets!

1,265. Become deeply involved in your church; don't just show up for Sunday services.

1,266. Examine how well you have done so far in dealing with your heartache. Vow to do even better in the future.

1,267. Beat your own drum. Toot your own horn.

1,268. Be a candle in the dark to others who are dealing with similar heartaches.

1,269. Purchase an entire new wardrobe.

1,270. Go to confession this week if you feel burdened.

1,271. Life is an exciting journey, and all that has happened is that you have hit a major or minor detour. Remember that, in time, your journey will be wonderful again.

1,273. Turn your breathing into a deep-cleansing ritual.

1,274. Remember holidays. Remind yourself to have fun.

1,275. Relax, relax, relax!

1,276. Heal your broken heart with a spiritual Band-Aid.

1,277. Right now, stop reading this book and go make plans for tomorrow night.

1,278. Turn your future over to God.

1,279. Act like yourself—only you can be you!

1,280. Prioritize your life. Make lists, charts, notes, graphs, or whatever it takes to help you get your life together.

1,281. See the glass as half full, not half empty.

1,282. Make a list of twenty things that you have accomplished in the past several years.

> *The sweetest revenge is to forgive.*
> ISAAC FRIEDMANN

1,283. Make a list of ten things that you have going for you.

1,284. Stand back from your problems and get a clear perspective on your troubles.

1,285. Give yourself a happy hour every day, where for a particular time period you promise yourself that you won't think of your troubles.

1,286. Be a law-abiding citizen. (Now is not the time to get into any kind of trouble.)

1,287. Strive to find the right balance between work and play.

1,288. Throw a coin in a fountain and make a wish for a brighter future.

1,289. Break your chains to the past.

1,290. Look for all the good going on all around you.

1,291. Face your limitations bravely.

1,292. Stretch like a cat to relieve your tensions.

1,293. Be like an old owl, and make only wise choices.

1,294. Never stop learning and growing, even if you are ninety years old!

1,295. Take pride in your work.

1,296. Learn the fine art of being able to apologize with grace and dignity.

1,297. When you feel like giving up, go deeper into your inner resources and reach down and try again.

1,298. Say your prayers with a childlike faith.

1,299. In your mind's eye, see yourself as a powerful, spiritual being.

1,300. Unclutter your life. Remember what good decorators have been telling us for years: "Less really is more."

1,301. Ride a stationary bike or work out on a treadmill when you can't get outdoors to work off your stress.

1,302. While waiting in a traffic jam, doctor's office, or airport, read a self-help book.

1,303. Make a list of ten places that you would like to visit, and then pick one. Plan to travel there this month.

1,304. Take a break in a sauna.

1,305. Make a list of ten childlike qualities that you admire. Now incorporate one or two of those into your personality.

1,306. When you make positive changes in your life, be wary of burning your bridges. You may need to cross back over them in the future.

1,307. Hold your shoulders back and your chin high. You are an important person and you want the world to see you that way.

1,308. On a lonely night, read the works of Henry David Thoreau.

1,309. Be your own best friend. Who else knows all about you?

1,310. Keep in mind that there are no exit ramps on the highway of life.

1,311. Don't shortchange yourself just because your self-esteem might be a little low at this time in your life.

1,312. Go on a safari. You can't feel sad while running from wild animals!

1,313. Embrace the unknown.

1,314. Make a list of all the people who have been in your shoes and succeeded.

1,315. Get psyched about the future.

1,316. Share your story with others.

1,317. Speak up at self-help meetings.

1,318. Start your spring cleaning even if it is the middle of November.

1,319. Give strength to others. Gain strength from others.

1,320. Joke, tease, and have a sense of humor about your predicament.

1,321. Plan an unusual adventure.

1,322. Be wary of finding happiness in a liquid or solid form.

1,323. Set about remedying your imperfections as soon as they surface if they are bothering you.

1,324. Form your own philosophy about life.

1,325. Organize your photos into albums and relive your happier times.

1,326. Know that there is a wonderful life waiting for you just around the corner.

1,327. Take a cross-country train ride.

1,328. Be curious.

1,329. Take action today to solve your troubles.

1,330. Live a graceful, rich life.

1,331. If you share a sorrow, you lessen
its impact to hurt.

1,332. Remember that love conquers
all. That sums it all up nicely!

1,333. Visit all the great natural
wonders of the world.

1,334. Resist the useless emotion of
being melancholy.

> *action may not always
> bring happiness,
> but there is no happiness
> without action.*
>
> BENJAMIN DISRAELI

1,335. Give up vanity and competition
in order to have a mended heart.

1,336. Don't make excuses.

1,337. Some people like to wear dark colors while they are feeling low, but others find it makes them feel drab and worse. Do what makes you feel good.

1,338. Play with little children on a playground.

1,339. Search for the silver lining in every cloud.

1,340. Listen to inspirational songs.

1,341. Belt out a fun song at a karaoke bar.

1,342. Spread hope and good cheer to everyone you meet today.

1,343. Always do what you know to be right.

1,344. Become a good listener to other people's troubles, and you will never be lonely again.

1,345. Turn the other cheek. Yes, you have to! Yes, even when it is very hard to do.

1,346. Start being productive and giving to the world around you.

1,347. Make the effort even when you don't want to.

1,348. Work to improve your mind.

Questions to Ask Yourself:
How can I solve this problem?
How can I make myself feel better?
Who can help me?
Where can I go to feel better?
What steps can I take to make
my life better?
What can I do
to ease my pain today?

1,349. Wander through a botanical garden.

1,350. Try role-playing with a trusted friend to get a different handle on your situation.

1,351. Look for the light at the end of the tunnel.

1,352. Try to make up quickly after an argument.

1,353. Write down ten of your favorite self-help quotes and read each one several times before you get out of bed in the morning.

1,354. Never listen to people who say, "I told you so."

1,355. If you pray for rain, know that you might just get some mud along the way.

1,356. Attend a workshop of interest to you.

1,357. Bake some heart-shaped cookies for yourself as a little treat.

1,358. Treat everyone you meet with respect. That includes yourself.

1,359. If you don't like being alone, start off by spending just a few minutes by yourself and then increase your time alone slowly over the next few months.

1,360. Take time to unwind when you get home from work at night.

1,361. Take a ride in a New York City taxicab, and for a brief period of time you will forget about all your other troubles.

1,362. Before you make any major change, examine all the far-reaching consequences.

1,363. Look for serendipitous events to happen in your life.

1,364. Understand that sometimes one of the best things you can do is admit defeat.

1,365. Keep your rooms well lit when you feel sad, to make your surroundings cheerier.

1,366. Give yourself time to cool off if you feel hot and testy!

1,367. Know that as long as you are living, you have an opportunity to cheer up.

1,368. Make your own good luck. You can do it, you know!

1,369. Remember that setbacks just make you stronger if your thoughts are in the right place.

1,370. Make a fun game out of your life.

1,371. Remember that healing comes from knowing the worst that can happen and accepting it if it can't be changed.

1,372. Stop planning your future by glancing back over your shoulder.

1,373. Fill your quiet hours with:
   Beautiful music
   A pet
   A great book
   A good movie

1,374. Just because you have had some form of heartache, don't let that make you into an alarmist.

1,375. Attend a pet parade and join in the fun.

1,376. Don't stop yourself from letting your feelings out except at an inappropriate time.

1,377. Plan a holiday party.

1,378. Get back into the game of life when you are ready, because sitting on the sidelines isn't nearly as much fun!

1,379. Speak uplifting phrases aloud to yourself throughout the day.

1,380. Imagine that you are seeing the world for the very first time.

1,381. When you feel a dose of self-pity coming on, do a kind gesture for someone else.

1,382. Ask a friend to give you little pep talks throughout the day.

1,383. Find comfort in the fact that you aren't the first, nor will you be the last, to feel sad.

1,384. Tonight, symbolically put an end to this painful chapter of your life by making some kind of grand gesture.

1,385. Realize that endings are just doorways to new beginnings.

1,386. Write your feelings in a letter to your therapist.

1,387. Tell your troubles to a stranger.

1,388. To feel close to nature:
Tend your garden
Take a nature walk
Go to the Grand Canyon
Swim in a stream

1,389. Get your endorphins working for you. A natural high can't be beat!

1,390. Remember that "sour grapes" are bitter. You can't enjoy them!

1,391. Call a mental time-out when you feel a case of the "grumpies" coming on.

1,392. Is life giving you lemons? Make lemonade!

1,393. Say a silent prayer when you are experiencing difficult moments away from home.

1,394. Spend the afternoon at a park feeding the birds to escape from the realities of everyday life.

*Experience is
a hard teacher because
she gives the test first,
the lesson afterwards.*
VERNON LAW

1,395. Open your home to others who are suffering.

1,396. Help is out there. Find out where you can go to get it.

1,397. Make a detailed description of how you would love your life to be. Now start to work on building that life.

1,398. View the planet as a wonderful, warm, safe, friendly place, and as you do your world will change for the better.

1,399. You are only human; don't expect to be perfect or to have a perfect life.

1,400. Want to know what you are really thinking? Start paying close attention to your moment-to-moment thoughts.

1,401. Explore a nature center.

1,402. When you make it through a particularly tough day, give yourself a reward.

1,403. Make the headlines in your local newspaper for performing an outstanding act of kindness.

1,404. Ask yourself what you need to do to change your sad mood to a happy mood, then do it.

1,405. Congratulate yourself every morning for making it through the night.

1,406. Remember, the good news about hitting rock bottom is that the only way to go is up!

1,407. Put a huge smile on your jack-o'-lantern.

1,408. Feeling fearful? It is a sign that you are alive and moving forward. Don't panic.

1,409. Release. Don't struggle.

1,410. Always use good manners
to add a touch of grace to
your life.

Maintain These Familiar Routines:
Mealtimes
Grooming habits
Sleep pattern
Customary dress
Social life

1,411. Try to become the earthly rock in
someone else's world.

1,412. When your friend is heartbroken,
sit and listen. Save your troubles
for later.

1,413. Spend your Saturdays helping
underprivileged kids.

1,414. Accept well-meaning, constructive criticism.

1,415. Read from the great spiritual
works every morning before you
get out of bed.

1,416. When you give, give from
the heart.

1,417. Fly a kite at your neighborhood park.

1,418. Seek out the right way to solve
your problems, which may not
be the path of your dreams.

1,419. Look for ways to help nature.

1,420. Play charades and act silly for a
change.

1,421. Stop gossiping about your friends'
hurts and disappointments.

1,422. Forgive anyone who has done you wrong, no matter how big the wrong. In fact, the larger the wrong, the more you need to forgive.

1,423. Pare down your possessions to create a more tranquil feeling in your environment.

1,424. Plan for tomorrow to be a worry-free day.

1,425. Accept any blame that has your name on it.

1,426. Have little meditation breaks throughout your day.

1,427. Make today a tear-free day. Yes, live on the edge and have fun!

1,428. Get up fifteen minutes earlier than usual and spend that time outdoors soaking up the fresh air.

1,429. Try to be polite under pressure.

1,430. When you turn your troubles over to God, don't take them back.

1,431. Change pessimism into optimism.

1,432. Ask your friends to help you get out of your rut.

1,433. Visit a zoo. There is something about being around animals that will lift your spirits.

1,434. Be direct in your approach to life and to healing.

1,435. Never confuse assertiveness with aggression.

1,436. Burn your favorite flavor of incense.

1,437. Realize that if you run from your troubles, they will only follow you.

1,438. Find someone who makes you feel hopeful about your future.

1,439. Be a human architect. Build yourself up.

1,440. If you need to make restitution, get busy.

1,441. Stop comparing yourself to celebrities.

1,442. Ask a prayer group to pray for you.

1,443. If you must fight a battle, go into it with a well-thought-out strategy.

1,444. Let go of every mental habit that holds you back.

1,445. Stop using labels for people and situations.

1,446. Mourn your losses today, so that your tomorrows will be happy.

1,447. Remember that bragging won't make you feel any better.

1,448. If the road that you are on isn't bringing you personal fulfillment, take a new path.

1,449. If you can't find your tears but know that you need to let your heartache out, listen to beautiful music that will move you to tears.

1,450. Make different choices about your life from now on.

1,451. Stop trying to bury your hurts. Work to get them out in the open.

1,452. Keep in mind that you are still a very special person in spite of your low spirits.

1,453. Give up the habit of self-doubt.

1,454. Every day of your life, find some quiet time to go within yourself.

Man, like the bridge,
was designed to carry the load
of the moment, not the combined
weight of a year at once.

WILLIAM A. WARD

1,455. Take one day off from work each week for the next month. Enjoy your vacation one day at a time.

1,456. Let life happen. Loosen up!

1,457. Plan to do something great and bold with your life.

1,458. Once you learn from your misfortunes, pass on your knowledge to others.

1,459. Do what you want to do. It is that simple!

1,460. Find a new role model each week until you are back on your feet.

1,461. Listen to opposing points of view on how to solve your troubles.

1,462. Set some new priorities for yourself.

1,463. Want to be a hermit? Well, you aren't alone. Here is a little list of well-known recluses:

Emily Dickinson
Hetty Green
James Mason
Henry Thoreau

1,464. Once you get into good physical shape, work at staying that way.

1,465. Practice self-awareness.

1,466. Watch for unexpected encounters that may show you solutions to your problems.

1,467. Define success in your own terms.

1,468. Accept your life with all its troubles as your own.

1,469. Do what is best for you as long as it doesn't hurt anyone else.

1,470. Let your faith help get you through your troubles.

1,471. Live to impress yourself.

1,472. Easy ways to pamper yourself:
    Buy your favorite foods
    Wear your good jewelry
    Buy yourself the best that
      money can buy
    Sleep on satin sheets

1,473. Take an emotional coffee break whenever you feel emotionally drained.

1,474. Give up trying to impress others.

1,475. Stop saying that you don't care when you really do care.

1,476. Plan a spontaneous day. It sounds silly, but it works wonders. Take a day each month that you leave open for chance, fun, and excitement.

1,477. Learn to be comfortable in your own skin.

1,478. Buy yourself a toy to play with this weekend. Some suggestions:
Teddy bear
Slinky
Frisbee
Doll
Board game

1,479. Stop negative thoughts the
minute they show up in your
mind. Don't let them take root
in your thinking.

1,480. Chase butterflies.

1,481. Stop blaming your parents for
your heartache. You are a
grown-up now and fully in
charge of your own life.

1,482. Don't allow bitterness to take up
residence in your soul.

1,483. Keep in mind that the best things
in life really are free.

*Resolve to keep happy, and
your joy and you shall
form an invincible host
against difficulty.*
HELEN KELLER

1,484. Remember that one day these will be the good old days. That should inspire you to live well.

1,485. You are not here to be a door-mat for others. Make sure they realize it.

1,486. Find inventive ways to solve old hurts.

1,487. Give without expecting anything in return and you will be much happier in the long run.

1,488. Take stock of all your assets.

1,489. Search out new resources to aid you at this crisis point in your life. Check out:

    Books
    Tapes
    Therapists
    Self-help groups

1,490. Remember: You usually regret the most what you don't do, not what you do.

1,491. Give yourself credit where credit is due.

1,492. Become your own Christopher Columbus and discover a whole new world for yourself.

1,493. Find the value in what life sends your way.

1,494. Don't let your heartache infringe on the joy in others' lives.

1,495. Do what you enjoy as often as you can, even if it seems silly to others.

1,496. Keep in mind that the clock is always ticking and that you are wasting valuable time feeling down in the dumps.

1,497. Put your imagination to work for you to build a better life for yourself.

1,498. Remind yourself during hard times that you know you can make it.

1,499. Give yourself a little gift on holidays to cheer up your spirits.

1,500. Buy an exotic pet to get some excitement back into your life.

1,501. Work on a beautiful and difficult jigsaw puzzle to keep your mind off your troubles.

1,502. Sing a happy tune in the shower.

1,503. Refrain from being a mental lightweight. Tackle tough, mind-enriching pursuits.

1,504. Do something to improve your health today. Examples:

> Quit smoking
> Exercise
> Stay out of the sun's harmful rays
> Lose weight

1,505. Be truthful. Be honest, especially with yourself!

1,506. Try to be agreeable even if you don't feel like Mr. or Ms. Congeniality.

1,507. Live a courageous life.

1,508. Keep in mind that time is a great healer.

1,509. Cultivate these qualities during painful times:

> Perseverance
> Tenacity
> Persistence

1,510. Skip down the street. Let everyone wonder what is up with you!

1,511. Look at mistakes as wonderful
opportunities to learn new ways
of looking at life.

1,512. If you feel that you can't eat,
drink a protein beverage to help
keep your strength up.

The lowest ebb
is the turn of the tide.
HENRY WADSWORTH LONGFELLOW

1,513. Understand that when we suffer
a loss in our lives it gives us a
great chance to reevaluate
what really holds meaning for us.

1,514. Whenever anyone lightens your
load, be sure to say thanks.

1,515. Hold firm to your convictions.

1,516. Make a list of any grudges you are holding. Now forgive each and every one of them.

1,517. Pack a gourmet picnic when you are feeling sad and head to your favorite, most picturesque spot.

1,518. Choose your companions very carefully. Sometimes our choice of friends should be reevaluated.

1,519. When you need to turn down a friend's request for emotional reasons, be firm.

1,520. Know that you are a spiritual be-ing having a human experience.

1,521. Help a child and you will auto-matically feel better. I suggest helping the Big Brothers/Big Sisters organization.

1,522. Ask God to be your copilot.

1,523. Clean out your clothes closet of anything that you haven't worn in two years. It will help you feel less cluttered.

1,524. Update your résumé. This might be a great time for a career change.

1,525. Have a big yard sale to get rid of all the junk you have around the house that you no longer want. It will give you a new lease on life to have your house in order.

1,526. Take full responsibility for yourself. Nobody likes the victim mentality.

1,527. Build yourself up emotionally before facing new and challeng- ing situations.

1,528. Live every single moment of your life. Know that the bad times just add flavoring and color.

1,529. Clean out your desk at the office to get a little better focus on work.

1,530. When you feel spontaneous and fun, act on the feeling before you lose it.

1,531. Visit Sea World and relish the opportunity to pet a dolphin.

1,532. Plan a surprise party for a friend.

1,533. Is there a disaster in your part of the country? Reach out to those in great need and you'll feel better immediately.

1,534. Recognize that you are already a success. You have made it this far in life!

1,535. Remember your happiest moments in life.

1,536. Look at the universe through a telescope for a moving experience.

1,537. Make amends. Your heart needs to be at peace to be fully recovered.

1,538. Learn to show your gratitude to others.

1,539. Define yourself by the type of person you are, not by your troubles.

1,540. Your pain will lessen with each sunrise, so look forward to each new day.

1,541. Make getting happy a number-one priority in your life.

1,542. Try to have at least one good friend who can always be counted on to be there for you when the chips are down.

1,543. Take it easy on those closest to you when your nerves are frayed.

1,544. Learn not to worry.

1,545. Take action!

The difference between stumbling blocks and stepping-stones is the way a man uses them.
AUTHOR UNKNOWN

1,546. Pick a bouquet of wildflowers.

1,547. Kiss and make up after a big fight.

1,548. Smile at someone every day. Start with:

Parents	Children	Siblings
Friends	Spouses	
Neighbors	Coworkers	

1,549. Join a worthwhile boycott.

1,550. Allow your dog to train you for a change.

1,551. Take a nap under the stars.

1,552. Take a half day off from work.

1,553. Be wary about becoming a workaholic if you are using work as a way to escape your sadness.

1,554. Do something that you love to do, in spite of your gloominess.

1,555. Even though you are feeling vulnerable, don't let yourself become too dependent on another human being for your emotional strength.

1,556. Make a detailed list of all the advice others have given you. Now look for which advice you can put to work.

1,557. Take your own informal survey of ways others have dealt with your type of heartache.

1,558. Attend a memorial service. You will have a new perspective on life by the end of the service.

1,559. Just because you are full grown doesn't mean that you should stop growing. Improve your skills.

1,560. Plant a tree in remembrance of a person or event.

1,561. Try to see that we are all in this together.

1,562. Stop being a perfectionist.

1,563. Work to create moments filled with wonder that you will remember for years to come.

1,564. Seek out the unfamiliar, the unknown, and the unusual.

1,565. Keep your vows.

1,566. Say grace at every meal.

1,567. Have a good conversation with yourself.

1,568. Plan to get to know yourself better than you know anyone else on this planet!

The man who
radiates good cheer,
who makes life happier
whenever he meets it,
is always a man of
wisdom and faith.
ELLA WHEELER WILCOX

1,569. Tell your best joke.

1,570. Rent an action movie like these
to get your mind off your troubles:
Twister
Speed
Die Hard

1,571. Yes, we do have a sixth sense,
and it is the one to pay the most
attention to at this particular
point in your life.

1,572. Take a busman's holiday in the
very near future.

1,573. Keep others' secrets.

1,574. Improve yourself by working with
an image consultant.

1,575. Try to schedule your work time
during your most productive
time period.

1,576. Meet your friends after work
instead of heading straight home.

1,577. Are you feeling nervous? Head out to the nearest Mexican restaurant and order a hot and spicy meal. It will cause your brain to produce more endorphins, and you will feel better.

1,578. Having trouble keeping your thoughts focused? Try eating fish—it will help your power of concentration.

1,579. Want to boost your energy? Drink lots of water.

1,580. What are your first thoughts on waking? Write them down and start learning from them.

1,581. Shake up your entire day to get a new lease on life.

1,582. Know that the more you do, the more energy you will create.

1,583. Read the writings of Thomas Moore.

1,584. Spend an evening reading *The Celestine Prophecy,* by James Redfield.

1,585. Give up trying to be perfect.

1,586. Love what you do for a living or change what you do.

1,587. Find something in your life to be enthusiastic about.

1,588. Ask for what you want in your prayers.

1,589. Sing your favorite hymn.

1,590. Work to bring others up, not down. By doing so, you'll raise yourself.

1,591. Practice random acts of kindness.

1,592. When you can't sleep, write in your journal.

1,593. Setbacks are a normal part of life. When you hit a roadblock, just take another route.

1,594. When you can't stand up for yourself, ask a friend to do it for you.

1,595. Know that we all fall before we can walk by ourselves.

1,596. Find joy and happiness in life's simple pleasures:

> Rain on a tin roof
> Falling stars
> Baking bread
> Freshly fallen snow

1,597. Work on solving your own troubles, before taking on someone else's.

1,598. Read the interesting book *Home for the Soul,* by Anthony Lawlor, to inspire you to create a beautiful home for yourself.

1,599. Spend at least fifteen minutes a day in prayer.

1,600. Empower yourself through prayer and meditation.

1,601. Wear a cologne that makes you feel attractive.

1,602. Delegate tasks to family and friends. You don't want to feel heartbroken and over-worked too.

1,603. Start a greenhouse, even if it has a very humble beginning.

1,604. Place fresh flowers in unexpected places to brighten up your world:
    Inside the refrigerator
    Around your bathtub
    In your car
    In the laundry room
    On your back porch

1,605. Entertain friends even when you are feeling down. You will start to feel better soon.

1,606. If you don't have a green thumb, buy silk flowers for your home.

1,607. Listen to a sermon by your favorite minister.

1,608. Visit your church library for books about dealing with heartaches and struggles.

The more difficult the obstacle, the stronger one becomes after hurdling it.

AUTHOR UNKNOWN

1,609. Turn off your TV and spend your time creatively.

1,610. Keep yourself out of traffic jams. You don't need that type of annoyance at this point in your life.

He is a wise man who
does not grieve for the things
which he has not,
but rejoices for
those which he has.

EPICTETUS

1,611. Read all the wonderful books by Peter Marshall.

1,612. Call the person who means the most to you and tell that person how you feel.

1,613. Practice your religion.

1,614. Don't sprint through your recovery period because you find it difficult.

1,615. Remember to bring flowers to the living.

1,616. When you feel unnerved, sit quietly in a rocking chair and listen to soft music.

1,617. Appreciate you!

1,618. Give up the tired excuse of saying you didn't know any better.

1,619. Play miniature golf with a friend.

1,620. Lose your worries while reading several newspapers from different cities.

1,621. Others can't know the entire scope of your pain, your life, your experience. Stop trying to share your experiences with everybody you meet.

1,622. Take a soul-cleansing walk in the rain.

1,623. Find a calling in life.

1,624. Consider changing your name
and moving to another city if
your troubles call for drastic
measures.

1,625. Practice the fine art of human
compassion.

1,626. Consider getting some house-
hold help if you feel over-
whelmed at home:
    Baby-sitter
    Companion
    Housekeeper
    Handyman

1,627. Go to a lovely flower shop and
treat yourself to the most beautiful bouquet in the shop.

1,628. Stop telling yourself what you
"should have done."

1,629. Mimic successful people.

1,630. Make a list of all the mottoes
and "truths" that you live by. Are
there any that need to be
changed?

1,631. Learn from nature.

1,632. Go on a whale-watching
expedition.

1,633. Know that you have the power
to choose your frame of mind.

1,634. Don't give a second thought
to how others view how you
handle your life.

1,635. You can change only circumstances, not other people.

1,636. Learn when to say enough is
enough!

1,637. Have a food fight with a loved one for a fun way to release tension.

1,638. Try to understand that other people cannot read your mind.

1,639. When you need to pour your heart out, tell a friend that you need some quality time with him or her. That lets the other person know what is required and what the person can expect of your time together.

1,640. Remember, going with the flow of life is much easier than swimming against the tide.

1,641. Even if you can't sleep, rest!

1,642. Read an enthralling mystery.

1,643. Look for God's handiwork everywhere you go.

1,644. Just because you make a mis-
       take doesn't mean you are a
       mistake!

1,645. Keep your expectations about
       your future realistic.

1,646. Memorize Saint Francis's
       famous prayer.

Life is a voyage
in which we choose neither
vessel nor weather,
but much can be done
in the management
of the sails and
the guidance of the helm.
Author Unknown

1,647. Never base your self-esteem on
       your career, social standing,
       material possessions, or marital
       status.

1,648. Start the next chapter of your life with a clean slate.

1,649. Let sleeping dogs lie.

1,650. Write down all the roles you play in life. Are there any that you want to change or even drop?

1,651. Imagine being a bird and soaring above your problems.

1,652. Understand that if you keep moving in the direction of your dreams, you will eventually reach them, even if you take small steps during the difficult periods of your life.

1,653. Stop the habit of doubting yourself.

1,654. Learn what God thinks about your particular struggles by reading the Bible.

1,655. Stay clear of arguments. You don't need any more stress than you are dealing with already.

1,656. Make up some light, happy fantasies. Try to make them become a reality.

1,657. Kiss your loved ones good night.

1,658. Listening to other people gripe is unproductive, so swear off it right this minute!

1,659. Treat yourself to dinner at a five-star restaurant.

1,660. Be with people who enhance and lift you up emotionally.

1,661. Know that your spiritual life is much more important than your material life.

1,662. Never allow others to coerce you into making a decision that doesn't feel right to you.

1,663. Guilt will stop you in your tracks. Get rid of it now.

1,664. Pray and then write down the answers you receive.

1,665. Listen to the beautiful and moving song "You'll Never Walk Alone."

1,666. Participate in a laughing contest.

1,167. Create a sense of joy everywhere you go.

1,668. Always be asking yourself how you can be happier.

1,669. Face the truth from the onset of your troubles. After all, you can fool yourself for only a little while.

1,670. Look for inspiration everywhere you go for the next twenty-four hours.

1,671. Consider taking your vacation in your own backyard.

1,672. Look for discernment and knowledge in the hearts of children.

1,673. Put your computer, fax, and telephone to good use by keeping in touch with out-of-town friends and family.

1,674. Browse through a wonderful art gallery and see the different perspectives that artists have of the world.

1,675. Create a home that feels like a safe haven for your soul.

1,676. Learn life lessons from the changing of the seasons.

1,677. Never say never.

1,678. You know the difference between right and wrong—you have since you were a child. Do what you know to be right.

1,679. Go to a big department store's major sale and treat yourself to a luxury item at a great bargain price.

1,680. Put a little beauty in your life by attending a large flower show.

1,681. Try to start your week off on a positive note such as accomplishing a special goal.

1,682. Stop yourself from flying off the handle, as it will only make your life worse.

1,683. Ask yourself if you are living the life that you had pictured for yourself.

1,684. When people hurt you, send them love.

1,685. Understand that positive energy attracts positive things to you. Negative energy attracts negativity to you.

1,686. You don't have to know everything. Ask experts for help.

1,687. When in doubt, choose the alternative that's most fun.

1,688. Laugh at your troubles.

1,689. Listen to the wise and wonderful lyrics of Walt Disney movie theme songs.

1,690. Read a self-help tip every day.

1,691. Be "real" with everyone you come in contact with each day.

1,692. Force yourself every day to:
     Get out of bed
     Get dressed
     Eat well
     Smile
     Rest
     Accomplish something

1,693. Create the highest vision for your life and start taking the necessary steps to achieve it.

1,694. Let your dog sleep on your bed, so when you wake up during the night you'll have someone to snuggle with and talk to.

1,695. Picture a beautiful scene in your mind, and mentally go there for an emotional rest period whenever life starts to get you down.

1,696. Look at the rose, not at the thorns.

1,697. Take up water-skiing or any activity
that needs your full concentration,
so that you can keep your mind
off your worries.

1,698. Think of your loved ones, living
and dead, and gain strength
from their love for you.

1,699. Count a different blessing every
day of your life. It will teach you
gratitude and optimism.

1,700. Find someone to inspire you.
Consider choosing:

A parent
Your boss
A minister
A national celebrity
A philosopher

1,701. Form your impressions of others
based on your own experience,
not someone else's.

1,702. Become a student of life.

Eight Proven Steps Toward
Feeling Better Fast:
Learn to accept change
Admit your weaknesses
Ask for any help that you
know you need
Be open to solutions
Deal directly with your problems
Admit your faults
Take full responsibility
for your heart
Tell the truth, especially
to yourself

1,703. Pessimism is a learned habit.
Give it up.

1,704. Find your own, unique way
to unwind.

1,705. Use your most prized possessions every day to enhance the quality and beauty of your world, instead of saving them, as most people do, to use for special occasions.

1,706. Act brave until you really feel brave.

1,707. Learn to be self-sufficient.

1,708. Make a list of ten romantic gestures that hold a special appeal for you. Then go and do one of these for yourself.

1,709. Set off fireworks to celebrate moving on with your life.

1,710. Find a favorite star and make a wish on it every night before you go to sleep until your heartache ends.

1,711. Read about UFOs.

1,712. Pray with your minister.

1,713. Expect the best.

1,714. Learn about yourself by trying new things, reading different authors, and doing things differently.

1,715. Stay clear of pessimistic people.

1,716. Be virtuous.

1,717. Look for the challenges, lessons, and excitement in the storms of life.

1,718. Force yourself to take risks that will change your world for the better.

1,719. Run barefoot through a park on a beautiful day.

1,720. Walk or ride a bicycle instead of driving whenever you can.

1,721. If you are feeling lost, look to heaven for direction.

1,722. Learn to be content with what you have in the world.

1,723. Research your family tree and think about the problems your ancestors must have faced.

1,724. Limit your responsibilities till you get back on your feet.

1,725. Just for today, decide to break any silly, useless rules in your life that make no sense to you.

1,726. Enjoy an afternoon of exploring along country back roads.

1,727. Prepare some of your favorite childhood snacks, such as S'mores and brownies.

1,728. Live by the concept that all of creation is sacred.

1,729. Always look at what others say
and do in the most positive light.
Give them the benefit of the
doubt. You will make yourself
much happier in the long run.

1,730. Accept your shortcomings. Just
for one day, give yourself the
benefit of the doubt.

1,731. Find a group of friends who are
willing to get together with the
goal of raising one another's self-
esteem and self-awareness.

1,732. Learn to look at your life in a
reflective manner. Try to be a
detective and understand your
motives.

1,733. Help ensure a better future in
another part of the world—
adopt an acre of South
American rain forest.

1,734. Stop making mountains out of molehills. Instead of:

> "disaster," say "disappointment"
> "catastrophe," say "nuisance"
> "horrible," say "disagreeable"
> "terrible," say "inconvenient"

1,735. When you state affirmations, be sure to say them with emotion and as much conviction as you can muster.

1,736. Keep in mind that everyone faces loss, aging, illness, personal setbacks, and loneliness.

1,737. Hire a paid companion to help you through your roughest times.

1,738. Make a reservation for the first spaceship to the moon.

1,739. Try to make a connection with at least one other person each day of your life.

1,740. Stop focusing on yourself and start looking out at the world and all the other people in it.

1,741. Listen to your body. What is it telling you? Do you feel relaxed or are you having stress-related problems such as headaches, tight muscles, or stomach upsets?

1,742. Keep a list of phone numbers of loved ones by your bed, to call when you feel especially lonely.

1,743. Make a list of five things that you need to do that would be interesting to you, and try to accomplish them during your low periods.

1,744. Treat yourself to an evening at the ballet.

1,745. Make happy memories for some-one else.

1,746. Check out health food stores for books on relieving tension. One technique to try is massaging the pressure points in your hands and feet.

1,747. Remember, there are always ways to change every situation; the key to success is finding the choices that will bring you the most happiness.

The happiest people are
those who think
the most interesting thoughts.

WILLIAM LYON PHELPS

1,748. When you feel as if you shouldn't do something fun or that you can't reach for the stars, stop and ask yourself, "Why not?"

1,749. When you feel that the whole world is talking about your mistakes or problems, look at a globe and realize that there are billions of people who don't even know about you or your troubles.

1,750. Work at being natural.

1,751. Speak from the heart. Say what you feel. Stop monitoring your words.

1,752. Let go of regrets.

1,753. Stop using profanity.

1,754. Try a yummy dessert. How about:

Cake	Ice cream
Cobbler	Mousse
Cookies	Napoleon
Custard	Parfait
Éclair	Pie
Glacé	Pudding

Are you tempted?

1,755. Keep in mind that self-love has no room for selfishness.

1,756. Accept your actions if you approve of them, and if not, change them.

1,757. When you want to make an affirmation stick in your mind, say it aloud.

1,758. Trust your gut feelings.

1,759. Be committed to overcoming all the obstacles in your path.

1,760. Work to save an animal on the endangered species list.

1,761. Free up your time. Take it easy for a while.

1,762. Plan to have some excitement in your life.

1,763. Listen to your favorite piece of music during your most stressful periods.

1,764. Consider that you may be suffering from chronic fatigue rather than a case of the blues. The symptoms are similar:

    Pale complexion
    Lack of spontaneity
    Tension throughout your body
    Anxiety
    Insomnia

1,765. Spend your bonus on a needy child.

1,766. Improve your standard of living.

1,767. Get your woes out in a profitable way: Paint a dark masterpiece or write a sad love song.

1,768. Slurp a big bowl of your mother's chicken soup.

1,769. Understand that faith in yourself will speed the healing process.

1,770. Change happens in different stages—look for unexpected turns and twists.

1,771. It is true that birds of a feather do flock together. If you want to be with happy companions, act happy; in turn, you will make yourself feel happier.

1,772. Learn to be a good listener, so that you'll never be lonely again. Here's how:

Don't tell your story, just listen
Lean toward the person talking
Ask questions
Never interrupt
Stop making judgments
Keep your eyes on the speaker

If you are a good listener, you'll have more friends.

1,773. Make a list of all your financial assets. You might just be surprised at your net worth.

1,774. Read a book from the *New York Times* best-seller list.

1,775. Visit patients in a nursing home to get your mind off your sorrows.

1,776. Shop for shut-ins and you'll appreciate your freedom.

1,777. Volunteer at a local hospital.

1,778. Mow the lawn of an elderly neighbor on a hot summer day.

1,779. Take an art appreciation class and start learning about all the beauty in the art world.

1,780. Keep in mind that vulnerability is an essential part of being alive.

1,781. Dance in a summer rain shower.

1,782. Choose to adopt an outlook of gratitude and appreciation.

1,783. Stop using the words "I hope." Don't say, "I hope things will be better." Instead say, "I know things will be better."

1,784. The more you test yourself, the stronger you will become.

1,785. Appreciate yourself just as you are now.

1,786. Make a winning bid at a charity auction.

1,787. Sell your unwanted CDs and books and use the money to buy yourself a special treat.

1,788. Optimists have a better quality of life, so get busy thinking happy thoughts.

Seek Professional Help If:

You have suicidal thoughts

*Your relationships are
beginning to suffer*

*You are still struggling
emotionally six months
after the initial heartbreak*

You have gained excessive weight

You feel sad constantly

*You are turning to drugs
or alcohol to ease your pain*

*You feel that your emotions
are blocked*

You feel stuck in a rut

*You have experienced
a significant loss*

*You do not have someone to
talk with about your hurt*

*You want professional help
but are afraid to go*

1,789. Treat your sadness as a call to try harder and live better.

1,790. Look for the humor in your situation—there has to be a little humor in it.

1,791. Rent a cabin up in the mountains for a great escape.

1,792. Worship at a charming country church.

1,793. Fill your heart with love instead of heartache.

1,794. When you grasp that each moment that you live is gone forever and you can't get it back, you will savor every opportunity and every relationship.

1,795. Jump up and down to release your frustrations.

1,796. Instead of looking down, look up.
Live your life this way.

1,797. Believe in:
Santa Claus
The Easter bunny
The tooth fairy

1,798. Ask yourself, "Who is writing the
script of my life?" If it isn't you,
make some major changes!

1,799. Ask yourself where you want to
be in six months. Write down your
thoughts.

1,800. Write down a list of twenty things
that you want to accomplish in
your lifetime. Why are you waiting to do these things? Get busy!

1,801. Keep in mind that your sad periods will pass, as most crying
spells last only ten minutes or less.

1,802. Right now, put down this book
and take a little break.

1,803. Work on protecting yourself from
similar heartaches in the future, if
possible.

> *The really happy man is the
> one who can enjoy the scenery
> when he has to take a detour.*
> AUTHOR UNKNOWN

1,804. Realize that your best is all you
can do—no more, no better.

1,805. Find out what your natural talents are and use them to gain
your heart's desire.

1,806. Make up your mind that you are
going to improve yourself in
some way today.

1,807. Stand back and ponder all the mysteries of life.

1,808. Earn the trust of those around you.

1,809. Your self-esteem will increase by doing. Get busy!

1,810. Pull your own weight. You will gain a sense of pride and accomplishment.

1,811. Get a face-lift.

1,812. Understand that you can be down but still have a spirit filled with joy.

1,813. Avoid people who are unkind, mean-spirited, or don't like you. You deserve to be treated with respect!

1,814. Visit a beautiful national park and enjoy the scenery.

1,815. Treat every day as if it were Thanksgiving. If you do, you will have a wonderful outlook on life.

1,816. Take an Alaskan cruise.

1,817. Treat every person you meet with dignity and grace.

1,818. Tell a funny story to your friends or family to cheer yourself up today.

1,819. Get into harmony with nature.

1,820. Make a list of your top three faults and then get busy getting rid of them.

1,821. Find a fun way to vent your frustrations.

1,822. Ask a friend to help you make some long-range plans for your future if you believe that you need some major changes.

1,823. Host a Bible study.

1,824. Remember that wherever you
        travel, you always take your
        same heart.

1,825. Support a humane society event.

1,826. Clean out the skeletons in
        your closet.

1,827. For absolutely no reason whatso-
        ever, throw a big bash.

1,828. Volunteer at a children's hospital.

1,829. Make a material gesture to
        honor a departed loved
        one. For example:

        Build a monument
        Donate medical equipment
          to a hospital
        Set up a scholarship fund
        Donate to a building fund

Ways to Cheer Up a Friend:
Give a copy of this book
Give gifts of homemade goodies
Provide child care
Send encouraging letters,
notes, faxes, telegrams
Listen
Hug
Spend time with
the hurting friend

1,830. Know within your heart that you
can handle anything that life
sends your way.

1,831. Let your guard down with
trusted friends.

1,832. Write a fabulous novel based on
your life story.

1,833. Don't build yourself up by tearing others down.

1,834. Take an aerobics class.

1,835. Improve your city by picking up litter.

1,836. Get into the habit of loving your neighbor.

1,837. This is basic, but needs to be said: Big boys do cry, and they should get those tears out of their system.

1,838. Tell neighborhood kids all your old knock-knock jokes.

1,839. Nurse a sick animal back to health.

1,840. Fish for compliments from close friends.

1,841. Make a meal out of your favorite appetizers.

1,842. Attend a charity bake sale and stock up on yummy goodies for late-night snacks.

If you don't get everything you want, think of the things you don't get that you don't want.

OSCAR WILDE

1,843. Write to a pen pal. People to People International will help you find a match.

1,844. Tape an uplifting motto to your bathroom mirror and ponder it each and every morning.

1,845. Run in a marathon.

1,846. Let love be the motive behind all your actions.

1,847. Treat yourself to an extravagant, once-in-a-lifetime gift.

1,848. Accept others just as they are and you will save yourself tons of needless torment.

1,849. Keep in mind that contentment is found within your own heart.

1,850. Write a love letter from the bottom of your heart.

1,851. Create a home and office environment that is light and airy.

1,852. Have friends of both sexes.

1,853. Work on creating healthy environments:
       Smoke-free
       Pollution-free
       Stress-free

1,854. Become a prayer junkie.

1,855. Run barefoot along a
sandy beach.

*Self-Help Groups to Look into to Help
Cheer You Up:*
Parents Without Partners
Al-Anon
Newcomer clubs
Bereavement groups
Disease societies

1,856. If you don't know what to
do next, stand back and
wait for guidance.

1,857. When you stumble—and you will
stumble—just pick yourself up
and go on.

1,858. Make a decision to say good-
bye to your bad mood on a
certain date.

1,859. Spend as much of your time as you can pursuing pleasurable activities.

1,860. Make a list of the ten best compliments you have ever received in your life and begin repeating them to yourself morning, noon, and night.

1,861. Don't give up on the world just because you have taken some very hard falls.

1,862. Turn yourself totally over to a very worthy cause.

1,863. Comfort your inner child.

1,864. If you are a city slicker, spend the day on a farm for a great change of pace.

1,865. If at first you don't make it, try again!

1,866. Play a game from your childhood, such as:

> Monopoly
> Clue
> Hide-and-seek
> Old maid

1,867. Keep in mind that true happiness can't be found in material
possessions.

1,868. Watch children at play.

1,869. Plan a major event for the very
near future.

1,870. Find a friend or family member
who will validate your feelings.

1,871. Improve your appearance by
taking the advice of a beauty
consultant.

1,872. Have a spiritual awakening.

1,873. Make it a heartfelt desire to live a tranquil, peaceful life.

1,874. Tell others all about the good things in your life. This will reinforce them in your own mind.

1,875. Never allow your feelings of self-pity to take root.

1,876. Keep to your regular sleep patterns as best as you can.

The Warning Signs of Depression:
Pessimistic outlook
Trouble concentrating
Loss of interest in life
Low energy level
Crying spells
Trouble sleeping

1,877. Take each of your problems one at a time.

1,878. Symbolically bury your troubles in piles of beautiful fall leaves.

1,879. Make the effort to get along with others, but most important, get along well with yourself.

1,880. Tired of your corporate job? Read Lisa Kivirist's *Kiss Off Corporate America* and start planning a life of personal and financial independence.

1,881. Make a scrapbook of your happiest times.

1,882. Have a fireside chat with a close friend.

1,883. Make a recipe for life that is nine parts happiness and only one part heartache.

1,884. Look for the goodness and kindness in others.

1,885. Help others to rebuild their lives after a major heartbreak.

1,886. Surprise yourself on August 7 (Chance Day).

Back of tranquillity lies always conquered unhappiness.
DAVID GRAYSON

1,887. Refrain from building your world around another person. Create a balanced life.

1,888. Never waste valuable time searching for answers that can't be found.

1,889. Remember that your tone of voice says much about your state of mind. So when you speak to others, use a pleasant tone of voice.

1,890. Even if it is the middle of the year, spend tonight making resolutions about your future.

1,891. Set some minigoals, so that when you accomplish them it will give you a little boost. Try:

Balancing your checkbook
Cleaning house
Walking a mile or two
Bathing the dog

1,892. Fix dinner early tonight, so that you can spend some extra time either working or visiting with a friend.

1,893. Sometimes the best thing to do when you feel sad is just to let the feeling wash over you and stay until it runs its course.

1,894. Have a picnic on the roof.

1,895. Make a sizable contribution to a worthy cause.

1,896. Don't overdo!

1,897. When you visit with friends, have "real" conversations.

1,898. Stop "tit for tat" thinking. It will only hurt you and make you bitter.

1,899. Think of times when you have learned the most. How do those times compare to now?

1,900. Get your friends and family to share their faith with you, and thereby strengthen your own.

1,901. Stop listening to family members and friends who say things can't be done.

1,902. Rate all the different areas in your life. Which ones are bringing you the most satisfaction? Pursue those areas with more gusto.

1,903. Never look back unless it is to reminisce or to learn.

1,904. Train your mind to think only those thoughts that will make you happier and healthier.

1,905. See your favorite singer in concert.

1,906. If things aren't going your way, take control by changing your strategies.

1,907. Make your own rules.

1,908. Send yourself a dream gift from a fabulous store by having the store's personal shopper pick out something tailored to your tastes.

1,909. Brighten up your world with:
    Bright clothes
    Balloons
    Colorful decorating
    Floral sheets

1,910. Spend a day at an amusement park.

1,911. Keep in mind that you are connected to every other person on the planet.

1,912. Browse a pet shop.

1,913. Cheer up those around you.

1,914. Watch a street magician perform.

1,915. Spend an evening building a gingerbread house that will delight the little ones during the holidays.

1,916. Throw your pennies into a wishing well and hope for the best.

1,917. Attend a circus and get caught up in the excitement of the big-top show.

1,918. Start adding some new, upbeat friends to your social life.

1,919. Understand that there is a spiritual solution to every single problem that you encounter.

1,920. Find a key pal on the Internet. You can start with www.cyber-friends.com.

1,921. Learn another language—and travel to a country where you can use it.

1,922. Make funny faces at yourself in the mirror.

1,923. Plant a living Christmas tree during the holidays.

1,924. Add one positive aspect to your life every week.

1,925. Live tomorrow as if you were on top of the world. What would you do? Do it!

1,926. Understand that when you change your heart, you change your mind. When you change your mind, you change your life.

1,927. Believe that you are lovable.

1,928. Believe that you are successful.

1,929. Refrain from jumping to conclusions about how everything will turn out in your life.

1,930. Live today as if it were your last.

1,931. Everywhere you go, look for friendly faces.

1,932. Be the master of your own fate.

1,933. Forgive and forget!

1,934. Treat yourself to a glamorous photo session with a professional photographer.

1,935. Get rid of your outdated ideas.

1,936. If you do any building, make sure it isn't a wall to keep others out of your heart.

1,937. Turn your world into a reflection of your inner tranquillity.

1,938. Perform a selfless act.

1,939. Clean all self-destructive thoughts out of your head.

1,940. Take your frustrations out on a
punching bag.

1,941. Travel around the world.

1,942. Take some dance lessons.

1,943. Be smart about your habits.
When you get rid of a bad habit,
fill the void with a good habit.

1,944. Write to our servicemen
and -women.

1,945. Look for your answers to come
sometimes in unusual ways.

*Learn from
the mistakes of others.
You can't live long enough to
make them all yourself.*

AUTHOR UNKNOWN

1,946. When you are able to give of yourself again, do so without strings attached.

1,947. For dinner tonight, how about eating an entire cheesecake instead of your usual meal of meat and potatoes?

1,948. Try to welcome solitude and to treat it as time spent with a friend.

1,949. Walk on the wild side—head to a Club Med resort.

1,950. Know the difference between solitude and loneliness.

1,951. You are unique. There is nobody in the world quite like you. Take advantage of this fabulous fact.

1,952. Treat yourself to an evening at the symphony.

1,953. Get an emotional checkup with a professional.

1,954. Brainstorm ways to help yourself. You will be happily surprised at all the good ideas that you have locked up inside your head.

1,955. Get into the wonderful habit of self-examination.

1,956. Remember that when you face your fears, they dwindle and often disappear.

1,957. Be generous in every way you can think of to others and to yourself.

1,958. Work on improving yourself every day of your life, even after your heart is healed.

1,959. Cut down on the amount of sugar you eat. Sugar drains you of energy after it gives you that initial boost.

1,960. Keep in mind that whatever you focus on grows in importance.

1,961. Learn to appreciate the simple joys found in your own part of the world.

Qualities of a
Fully Recovered,
Formerly Sad Person:

Openness	*Spontaneity*
Joyfulness	*Self-sufficiency*
Peacefulness	*Lovingness*
Kindness	*Spirituality*

1,962. Look deep inside to find even the tiniest drop of enthusiasm that is locked within your heart. Use it to bring yourself back to a happy state of mind.

1,963. Visit the countries that your ancestors came from.

1,964. Remember that you are a spiritual being, and one day you will be going home. In other words, your problems are only temporary.

1,965. Keep in mind that your greatest spiritual growth usually comes in moments of solitude.

1,966. Lose your troubles in the beautiful music of an opera.

1,967. Stroll down an unfamiliar path in the woods.

1,968. The best foods for healing a broken heart:

    Chocolates
    Pizza
    Hot chocolate
    Ice cream
    Homemade cookies
    Lobster (just because you
      deserve it)

1,969. If nights are a lonely time, throw a slumber party or at least invite a friend to stay over with you.

1,970. Remember that slow and steady always wins the long race.

1,971. Put yourself first for a change.

1,972. Read the entertainment section of your newspaper for ideas on where to go and what to do in your spare time.

1,973. Love God, yourself, and others (in that order).

1,974. Travel to a different culture even if it is only as far as a different ethnic area of your city. It may give you a different perspective on your life.

1,975. Go on an adventure of a lifetime, such as a trip to a South Sea island.

1,976. For good companionship, create your own "dream" family outside of your blood relatives.

1,977. Take some lessons, such as:
Swimming
Painting
Golf
Tennis

1,978. Become a member of Welcome Wagon and start meeting lots of new people.

1,979. Leave every person you come into contact with feeling better after having spent time with you. In turn, you will start to feel better.

1,980. Hang a beautiful painting where you will see it every day and it will brighten your spirits.

1,981. Don't give up the joy of sex in your marriage.

1,982. Take a stress-management class to learn how to relieve your tension.

1,983. Give yourself some sweet rewards for every hurdle that you get over. Consider rewards such as:

Gold jewelry
Pearls
A great book
A trip
Gourmet foods
A show-class puppy

1,984. Buy a full body pillow to take your stress out on or to cuddle up with on a lonely night.

1,985. Buy a CD of Celtic music and let it sweep you away to another time and place.

1,986. Keep your feet firmly on the ground but your head up in the clouds.

1,987. Put pleasure, happiness, and joy first. Put duty second for a change.

1,988. Eat dinner in bed for a lazy change of pace.

1,989. Know that happiness is just around the corner.

1,990. Ask your mother to tape-record some lullabies to help you fall asleep on lonely nights.

1,991. Find a refuge from the storm that works for you.

1,992. Pray on your knees and you will feel closer to God.

1,993. Rock a child to sleep in your arms.

1,994. Step out in faith, trusting in God to be your guide.

1,995. Turn your world around just by:

> Speaking the right words
> Making a house a home
> Turning a meal into a feast
> Viewing life as a journey
> Making a pet a companion
> Turning a business trip into an adventure
> Making a friend out of a stranger
> Turning a day off into a holiday
> Looking at a problem as a test

1,996. Find your authentic self. Who are you deep down inside? Once you know the real you, you will be better able to know what will make you feel better.

1,997. Learn from animals how to:

> Live for the moment
> Take things as they come
> Care for their families
> Enjoy the basics: pretty days, good health, and good food

1,998. Find a good read for those times that you just can't sleep or when you need some companionship but your friends aren't available.

1,999. Know that pain, struggle, and loss are three of the best teachers you will ever have!

2,000. Find refuge in your church.

2,001. Ways to find out if you have found closure to your downtime. Ask yourself:

Am I suffering from fears stemming from the hurt?
Do I overeat?
Do I drink too much?
Have I come to terms with the cause of my broken heart?
Am I hiding my true emotions?
Have I learned the "lesson" from my experience?

2,002. Go through this book and circle all the ways that you know will help *you* to cheer up, and then start doing them.

I have found that most people are about as happy as they make up their minds to be.

ABRAHAM LINCOLN